Cambridge Elements

Elements of Sustainability: Science, Policy, Practice
edited by
Series Editor-in-Chief
Arun Agrawal
University of Notre Dame

ON THE GLOBAL WATER CRISIS

A Taxonomy of Human–Water Challenges

Paulina Raniecka
Vrije Universiteit Amsterdam

Nikolas Galli
Polytechnic University of Milan

Camilla Govoni
Polytechnic University of Milan

Maria Cristina Rulli
Polytechnic University of Milan

Sergio Villamayor-Tomas
Autonomous University of Barcelona

Jampel Dell'Angelo
Vrije Universiteit Amsterdam

Shaftesbury Road, Cambridge CB2 8EA, United Kingdom

One Liberty Plaza, 20th Floor, New York, NY 10006, USA

477 Williamstown Road, Port Melbourne, VIC 3207, Australia

314–321, 3rd Floor, Plot 3, Splendor Forum, Jasola District Centre, New Delhi – 110025, India

Cambridge University Press is part of Cambridge University Press & Assessment, a department of the University of Cambridge.

We share the University's mission to contribute to society through the pursuit of education, learning and research at the highest international levels of excellence.

www.cambridge.org
Information on this title: www.cambridge.org/9781009658812

DOI: 10.1017/9781009658850

© Paulina Raniecka, Nikolas Galli, Camilla Govoni, Maria Cristina Rulli, Sergio Villamayor-Tomas, and Jampel Dell'Angelo 2026

This publication is in copyright. Subject to statutory exception and to the provisions of relevant collective licensing agreements, no reproduction of any part may take place without the written permission of Cambridge University Press & Assessment.

When citing this work, please include a reference to the DOI 10.1017/9781009658850

First published 2026

A catalogue record for this publication is available from the British Library

A Cataloging-in-Publication data record for this Element is available from the Library of Congress

ISBN 978-1-009-65881-2 Hardback
ISBN 978-1-009-65886-7 Paperback
ISSN 2635-0211 (online)
ISSN 2635-0203 (print)

Additional resources for this publication at www.cambridge.org/raniecka-et-al

Cambridge University Press & Assessment has no responsibility for the persistence or accuracy of URLs for external or third-party internet websites referred to in this publication and does not guarantee that any content on such websites is, or will remain, accurate or appropriate.

For EU product safety concerns, contact us at Calle de José Abascal, 56, 1°, 28003 Madrid, Spain, or email eugpsr@cambridge.org

On the Global Water Crisis

A Taxonomy of Human–Water Challenges

Elements of Sustainability: Science, Policy, Practice

DOI: 10.1017/9781009658850
First published online: February 2026

Paulina Raniecka
Vrije Universiteit Amsterdam

Nikolas Galli
Polytechnic University of Milan

Camilla Govoni
Polytechnic University of Milan

Maria Cristina Rulli
Polytechnic University of Milan

Sergio Villamayor-Tomas
Autonomous University of Barcelona

Jampel Dell'Angelo
Vrije Universiteit Amsterdam

Authors for correspondence: Paulina Raniecka, p.raniecka@vu.nl and Jampel Dell'Angelo, jampel.dellangelo@vu.nl

Abstract: The threat of an impending global water crisis has proliferated across water governance literature in the recent decades. However, defining the nature of this global water crisis remains a challenge, as a plethora of problems fall under this term. Simultaneously, contemporary waterscapes are hard to navigate due to the interconnected and wicked nature of water issues. Thus, to unravel this complex picture, it is fundamental to be reflexive about how water problems are identified, defined, and addressed. Conducting a systematic literature review and applying a constant comparative method, this Element identifies nine key human–water problématiques. Additionally, the analysis traces co-occurrences between diverse problématiques and their conceptual subclusters. Based on exhaustive literature, a reflection on the complex issue of 'what solutions?' is elaborated. Lastly, contributions to the ontological question of what a water problem is are offered, indicating a transition beyond an understanding of water issues as solely tangible.

Keywords: water governance, sustainability, water crisis, human–water problématiques, taxonomy of water problems

© Paulina Raniecka, Nikolas Galli, Camilla Govoni, Maria Cristina Rulli, Sergio Villamayor-Tomas, and Jampel Dell'Angelo 2026

ISBNs: 9781009658812 (HB), 9781009658867 (PB), 9781009658850 (OC)
ISSNs: 2635-0211 (online), 2635-0203 (print)

Contents

1 Introduction   1

2 Methodology   5

3 Identifying Human–Water Problématiques   10

4 Discussion   39

5 Conclusion   45

References   47

An Online Appendix for this Element is available at www.cambridge.org/raniecka-et-al

1 Introduction

References to the threat of an impending global water crisis have proliferated in the recent decades, suggesting devastating developments looming in the near future (e.g., Biswas & Tortajada, 2019; Dellapenna et al., 2013; Jury & Vaux, 2005, 2007; Moe & Rheingans, 2006). The concept of the 'global water crisis' has become increasingly present within academic literature since the early 1960s, with the number of documents published per year growing steadily, particularly since the turn of the twenty-first century (Biswas & Tortajada, 2023). Despite these trends, defining the nature of this global water crisis remains a challenge, as a plethora of water problems have fallen under the umbrella of this term (Srinivasan et al., 2012). Simplistically defined as a set of pressures to the global water reserves, the global water crisis encompasses an array of issues. This global waterscape is hard to navigate, as water problems are characterized by interconnectivity and reciprocity. The innate complexities of water as a resource, society's relationship to it, and its centrality for all ecosystems emphasize the wicked nature of contemporary water issues (Brennan et al., 2021; Cooley et al., 2013; Jury & Vaux, 2007; Li, Endter-Wada, & Li, 2015; Rangecroft et al., 2021; Woodhouse & Muller, 2017).

The global water crisis has been more recently redefined as a crisis of governance (Biswas & Tortajada, 2023; Cooley et al., 2013). According to this perspective, the mainstream water governance practices are ill-equipped to effectively cope with the swelling pressures imposed on water resources (Dellapenna et al., 2013). In this view, despite numerous efforts over the last decades, water challenges remain unresolved due to insufficient action and the debilitating effect of problem complexity on policy delivery (Cooley et al., 2013; Dellapenna et al., 2013; Grigg, 2021; Kirschke et al., 2017). The need for innovative and more robust governance practices has been stipulated within the water governance literature over the years (e.g., Baird et al., 2015; Cooley et al., 2013; Dellapenna et al., 2013; Jury & Vaux, 2007). Global water governance needs to take a leap to adopt practices better suited for the current challenges, as the growing pressures on water resources have been heightening at an alarming speed, particularly in recent years, with research showing that the world is off-track for meeting the Sustainable Development Goals for water by 2030, following in the steps of the unmet targets of the Millennium Development Goals (MDGs) set at the turn of the century (Hove et al., 2019; Koehler, 2023; Vörösmarty et al., 2010).

In the words of Jury and Vaux (2007), "the problems are daunting, but we are not without the means to address them" (p. 69). Nonetheless, despite the existence of an abundance of scientific information relevant in the face of current water crisis, the data are not being applied (Graffy, 2006; Grigg, 2021; Jury & Vaux, 2005; Pahl-Wostl, 2017). The key limitation is the lack of a general consensus or any form of an overview of what actually constitutes the 'global water crisis,' neither from an academic nor a practitioner point of view. This diversity in perceptions displays that one's definition of water (and thus water problems) is highly contextual and dynamic, reflecting the multiplicity of water's material and elusive forms (Macura-Nnamdi & Sikora, 2023). Linton (2010) suggests a relational perception of water, arguing that it is the "various things and circumstances that . . . make water what it is" (p. 30). At the same time, there appears to be an absence of synthesis among global assessments on urgent water challenges, reflected in the continuous (re-)formulation of "challenges that are all variations and specifications of a limited set of problems" (van der Zaag, Gupta, & Darvis, 2009, p. 905). Exhaustive overviews of human–water problems discussed in academic literature have received little attention. There are a few exceptions, such as the research conducted by Srinivasan et al. (2012) on syndromes of coupled human–water issues, the study by Vörösmarty et al. (2010) on threats to river systems globally, publication on water governance paradigms by Bilalova, Newig, & Villamayor-Tomas (2025), and papers on global water grabbing (e.g., Dell'Angelo, Rulli, & D'Odorico, 2018; Franco, Mehta, & Veldwisch, 2013; Rulli, Saviori, & D'Odorico, 2013) and on the global virtual water trade (e.g., D'Odorico et al., 2019; D'Odorico, Dell'Angelo, & Rulli, 2019; Hoekstra & Chapagain, 2011). However, to the knowledge of the authors, there is no comprehensive study that synthesizes the abundance of literature on human–water problems globally.

Moreover, ambiguity in the way water discourses are applied by different actors brings political and power implications (Fallon, Lankford, & Weston, 2021). A leading example is the introduction of the interchangeably used notions of 'global water commons' and water as a 'global common good,' repeatedly adopted in the documents leading up to the United Nations (UN) 2023 Water Conference and during the event itself. An undoubtedly historic event, the Conference took place nearly 50 years after its predecessor – the 1977 UN Water Conference in Mar del Plata – the first ever water conference at a global scale (Quentin Grafton et al., 2023). Despite an inclusion of a variety of voices, it was arguably the highly visible involvement of corporate actors that was particularly noted (Mehta & Nicol, 2023; Sojamo & Rudebeck, 2024). In his analysis of the 2023 Conference, Vinciguerra (2024) demonstrates that despite the reliance on common vocabulary, the used concepts carry divergent meanings (and intentions) depending on the actor. In particular, Vinciguerra emphasizes two subgroups based on their understanding of a 'common good' – one relying on neoliberal economic theory of the commons and the other in favor of wider public involvement.

In a similar vein, D'Odorico et al. (2024) critically reflect on this representation of water resources, raising concerns about the manipulation of this term to create the conceptual preconditions for privatization and commodification of water, and the leading role of the market as the best way to solve a potential 'Tragedy of the Commons.' This concern is also raised by Puy and Lankford (2024), who scrutinize the narratives used by the recently established Global Commission on the Economics of Water (GCEW) in reference to the ongoing water crisis. Convened by the government of the Netherlands and facilitated by the Organization for Economic Cooperation and Development (OECD), the Commission promises the development of "new thinking" (GCEW, 2023, para. 4) in the face of the ongoing standstill within the water policy and governance arena. Relying on a one-dimensional conceptualization, GCEW's understanding of the water crisis risks the return to panacean prescriptions and singular, paradigmatic thinking (Puy & Lankford, 2024). What is more, the line of thinking advocated for by the GCEW is unsurprisingly heavily reliant on market-based management of water resources, attaching monetary valuation and pricing prescriptions.

This review recognizes the need to go beyond a reductionist understanding of water problems, acknowledging the diverse ways water (and water challenges) are perceived. We believe that there is a clear need to identify and examine (human-)water problems in a broader and integrated manner. While partial, the linkages between diverse water problems are visible, with an ever-growing body of water governance literature describing the synergies and interdependence among water issues (see, e.g., Brennan et al., 2021; Jury & Vaux, 2007; Li, Endter-Wada, & Li, 2015; Woodhouse & Muller, 2017).

Water problems are wicked. They are complex, multi-dimensional, and unsolvable through the use of conventional, linear approaches (Lach, Rayner, & Ingram, 2005; Markowska et al., 2020; Rittel & Webber, 1973; Sanya, 2020). As wicked problems, they are difficult to define and "essentially unique" (Rittel & Weber, 1973, p. 164). Therefore, their solutions are hard to delineate and implement, as they carry both short- and long-term consequences (Grafton, 2017; Sanya, 2020). What is more, each wicked problem could be viewed as a symptom of another issue (Rittel & Weber, 1973). Thus, wickedness stems partially from the inherent interconnectedness of problems, something that evidently gets in the way of a simplistic taxonomic representation.

Nevertheless, in order to provide some analytical meaning to the ambiguous notion of 'global water crisis,' this research embarks upon an examination of academic literature and careful identification of emerging human–water 'problématiques' – meta-problems that go beyond the specific closed and clearly delineated definition of 'problems' and can be generalized as coherent areas of research and policy intervention even when happening on multiple spatial and governance scales.

Building on the concept of a 'problématique' introduced by Ozbekhan (1970) in the proposal for the Club of Rome, we define a problématique within the space of water challenges as a cluster of similar types of water problems; a broader, higher-level, recurring issue that manifests on multiple scales in various geographical settings, and persists in time. For the purpose of this Element, water challenges are understood as specifically human–water problems that represent a threat, an obstacle, a reason for concern or fear, and for which solutions are being searched or should be searched.

The focus on human–water problems stems from the fact that water challenges have both humans and nature at their heart, as shown by the interconnection between social and hydrological systems (Rangecroft et al., 2021). Furthermore, wicked problems are believed to always occur in a social context, with water problems more specifically often weaving "water and society together in a way that no single root cause of related complexity, uncertainty, or disagreement can be discerned" (Fallon, Lankford, & Weston, 2021, p. 36; Lach, Rayner, & Ingram, 2005).

Effective water governance practices require coordination between diverse actors, sectors, and scales, coupled with the agenda alignment (Cooley et al. 2013). Applying a synthesizing lens would allow for a clear delineation of the most pressing human–water challenges, helping set priorities for future-oriented water governance and effectively communicate the challenges of the ongoing water crisis with policymakers, practitioners, and the wider society. It is fundamental to be reflexive and critical about how water problems are identified, prioritized, and addressed, as these processes have political and decision-making implications. At the same time, unpacking the concept of the global water crisis can lead to more guided action, with a clearer focus and intention allowing for effective water governance practices.

This research engages with a synthesis of academic literature to produce a taxonomy of human–water problématiques and their components, and to develop a glossary for the global water crisis, contributing to the concretization of the question of *what we talk about when we talk about the global water crisis*. The Element examines: (1) what the most pressing contemporary human–water problématiques are according to the water governance scholarship; (2) how these problems are conceptualized by different scholars; (3) how the identification of human–water problématiques impacts the generation of water governance paradigms, water governance patterns, and solutions; and (4) to what extent trends in prioritization of certain human–water problems over the years can be observed.

To address these questions, this Element relies on a two-step methodology, consisting of a systematic literature review (SLR) and a constant comparative method (CCM). This review is organized in the following manner: Section 2 discusses the applied methods. Section 3 presents the main results of this Element; first, in the form of a taxonomy, and second, as an in-depth water governance glossary, where each cluster represents a human–water problématique and its components. Section 4 discusses the linkages between distinct problématiques, reflects on potential solutions mentioned in the analyzed body of literature, and traces the evolution of the term 'problem' in the water governance scholarship. Lastly, the Conclusion completes the Element with some final remarks and thoughts about the way forward.

2 Methodology

The methodology applied in this research was twofold. The first phase applied an SLR as a means of collecting and reviewing existing scientific data on human–water problems worldwide to arrive at an overview of problématiques. The database created through this process served as the foundation for the second stage of the methodological approach – a constant comparative analysis centered around the objective of creating a water governance glossary. The following sections dive into the specific steps of the two stages.

From a theoretical stance, the point of departure for this research is the underlying recognition of water problems as wicked. Standing in opposition to tame problems, wicked issues cannot be tackled through 'normal science.' Therefore, this research is rooted in the 'post-normal science' (PNS) approach. This is applicable in cases where "facts are uncertain, values in dispute, stakes high, and decision urgent" (Funtowicz & Ravetz, 1994, p. 1882). Considering the wickedness of water problems, a conventional understanding of those as issues in need of clear, definitive solutions does not seem to be accurate (Fallon, Lankford, & Weston, 2021; Funtowicz & Ravetz, 1994). Moreover, the relevance of PNS in this context is further strengthened by its applicability in face the of epistemological uncertainty, a concept particularly relevant for this research (Funtowicz & Ravetz, 1993).

Considering the large scope of this research, an engagement with divergent theoretical approaches, paradigms, and epistemological diversity was expected. At the same time, a visibilization of the existent plurality of worldviews and knowledges was one of the ambitions of this work. Therefore, this Element simultaneously draws on social constructivism, which recognizes the crucial influence of the wider context on one's perception (and construction) of reality (Amineh & Asl, 2015; Fallon, Lankford, & Weston, 2021). As shown by this research, the numerous understandings of reality translate into the many definitions of water and, by extension, water problems (Macura-Nnamdi & Sikora, 2023).

As argued by the PNS approach, a dialogue involving all voices is needed to reach effective solutions (Funtowicz & Ravetz, 1993). This research makes a step toward this goal by engaging with a pluriverse of perspectives within the water governance scholarship, veering away from reductionist approaches and the idea of one, universal way of understanding the global water crisis.

2.1 Systematic Literature Review

This research applies an SLR approach to: (1) perform a coherent search strategy with the objective of identifying all relevant publications within the water governance scholarship; and to (2) facilitate a synthesis of the findings (Moher et al., 2015). The conducted literature review is molded according to the PRISMA (Preferred Reporting Items for Systematic Reviews and Meta-analyses) protocol.

2.1.1 Data Sources

To narrow down the number of potential publications and to ensure a high quality and relevance of included sources, SCOPUS was used as the sole database. Although problématiques refer to higher-level issues that manifest on multiple scales and in various geographical settings, for operational reasons, the review was restricted to English-language publications. Nonetheless, the authors recognize the value of expanding the data sources to different languages, as reliance on exclusively English-language literature could lead to a Western bias and a neglect of alternative perspectives, including those originating from the Global South. Thus, the literature sources are treated with consideration for this aspect.

2.1.2 Search Strings

For the purpose of this Element, a single search string including an exhaustive number of related search terms was preferred over the use of several search strings in parallel. This choice was selected based on the expected increased efficiency. In the trial phase, a search string consisting of terms "water," "governance," and "problem*," followed by synonyms to each component was applied. However, this process offered 47,753 sources, which were then narrowed down through different search iterations. Ultimately, a search string consisting of a list of terms synonymous with "water," followed by "governance" AND "problem*" was selected.

With the aim of identifying all the human–water problems discussed in the academic literature, this research is of an explorative nature. Thus, to remain unbiased when conducting the database search, search terms that might suggest a specific water-related problem and nudge the process onto a specific trajectory were omitted. Therefore, the authors refrained from including terms such as "pollution" or "water conflict*" in order not to manipulate what kind of articles the search would yield. The final search string consisted of a list of purely water/hydrologic terms synonymous to "water" based on the expertise of the interdisciplinary group of academics working on this research. After several iterations and interdisciplinary discussions, the authors arrived at the following search string:

> water* OR freshwater* OR groundwater* OR river* OR basin* OR watershed* OR catchment* OR irrigation* OR wastewater* OR wetland* OR lake* OR hydro* OR glacier* OR sociohydro* OR aquatic* OR "urban water" OR desalinat* OR ecohydro* OR reservoir* OR dam* OR hydropower OR rain* OR precipitation OR runoff OR "overland flow" OR "transboundary" AND governance AND problem*

2.1.3 Eligibility Criteria

To narrow down and increase the robustness of the potential literature, specific eligibility criteria were applied when searching the selected database. These are listed in Table 1.

Table 1 An overview of eligibility criteria applied in the conducted SLR.

	Eligibility criteria
Focus of the publication	freshwater governance problems
Date of publication	between 2004 and 2022
Language	English
Document type	peer-reviewed scientific articles from indexed journals
Geographic location	global

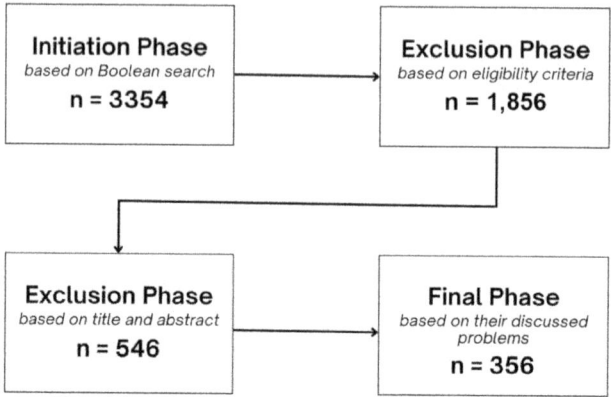

Figure 1 The process of study selection for the review.

2.1.4 Study Selection

A total of 1,856 publications for potential inclusion were obtained through SCOPUS using the selected search string and applying the eligibility criteria. Subsequently, the titles and abstracts were screened for relevance. The final selection was made over three sessions, where the researchers made a collective decision on the inclusion or exclusion of each of the shortlisted sources (see Figure 1). The final number of publications included for coding totaled at 546, while the total used for this research added up to 356 (Appendix A). The selection process was based on the discussed problem each paper centered around.

2.1.5 Coding and Data Aggregation

Having selected the final pool of sources, each of the publications was coded according to the problem(s) they discussed. The identified issues were subsequently clustered. This step was twofold, with issues first classified according to larger umbrella themes they fall under (e.g., water quantity), and further divided according to their specific focus (e.g., water scarcity, water stress, and water shortage). This process resulted in a creation of an overview of human–water problems as shown in academic literature of the past 18 years.

2.2 Constant Comparative Method

As the second step of the methodology, this research applied the constant comparative method to inform the process of identifying human–water problématiques. It is a tool for analyzing qualitative data through coding and synthesizing the available information inductively (Memon, Umrani, & Pathan, 2017). This process

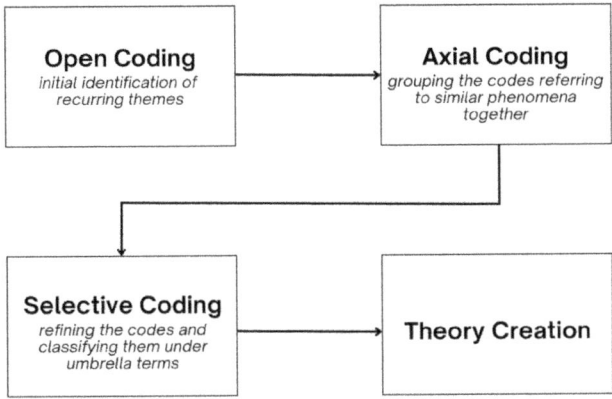

Figure 2 An overview of steps of CCM.

is based on a systematic reduction of sources into codes and a further derivation of themes from the codes, following inductive reasoning (Onwuegbuzie, Leech, & Collins, 2012). Accordingly, the derived codes and themes are to be grounded in the analyzed data rather than in preconceptions dictated by a pre-established conceptual framework (McGhee, Marland, & Atkinson, 2007). In that sense, this process calls for constant reflexivity by the researcher.

Following the original steps of the CCM (see Figure 2), the first stage includes open coding where initial identification of recurring themes takes place (Memon, Umrani, & Pathan, 2017; Onwuegbuzie, Leech, & Collins, 2012). In this research, this phase was referred to as the first-layer coding, where four researchers coded each of the shortlisted sources based on the problem typology they discussed. Each of these codes used the exact phrasing of the authors of a given study. The second step revolved around preliminary synthesis, where codes referring to similar phenomena were grouped together. After revising the assigned codes, each created category was assigned an umbrella term (i.e., a problématique). This final step of data refinement concludes with a creation of a theory out of the data (Onwuegbuzie, Leech, & Collins, 2012). In this Element, this step takes the shape of a human–water taxonomy, presented both visually and in the form of a water governance glossary.

The purpose of the water governance glossary is to describe each problématique and its components with the help of illustrative scientific literature. To identify optimal sources, the researchers conducted a second round of literature search in SCOPUS with targeted search strings for each subcomponent (e.g., "non-point source" OR "nonpoint source" OR "diffuse source" AND pollut* AND *water AND PUBYEAR > 2003 AND PUBYEAR < 2023). First, we checked whether the sources listed in the given subcluster of our database appeared in the SCOPUS list obtained through the targeted search. Second, we listed the top five most cited sources from SCOPUS relevant for our research. Lastly, a combination of five sources retrieved from both our problématiques database and the targeted search was used to inform each section of the water governance glossary. The selection process can be seen in detail in Appendix B.

3 Identifying Human–Water Problématiques

Taking a sample of 546 sources, this study resulted in the identification of nine human–water problématiques. Those problématiques are bundles of similar types of problems, here referred to as 'subclusters.' Most of those bundles consist of several subclusters constituting a problématique (see Figure 3). The identification of human–water problems was the result of the SLR, performed by three researchers. Consecutively, applying CCM as the method, the array of problems was further scanned in search of themes, which then became subclusters. This process was repeated to arrive at the final list of human–water problématiques.

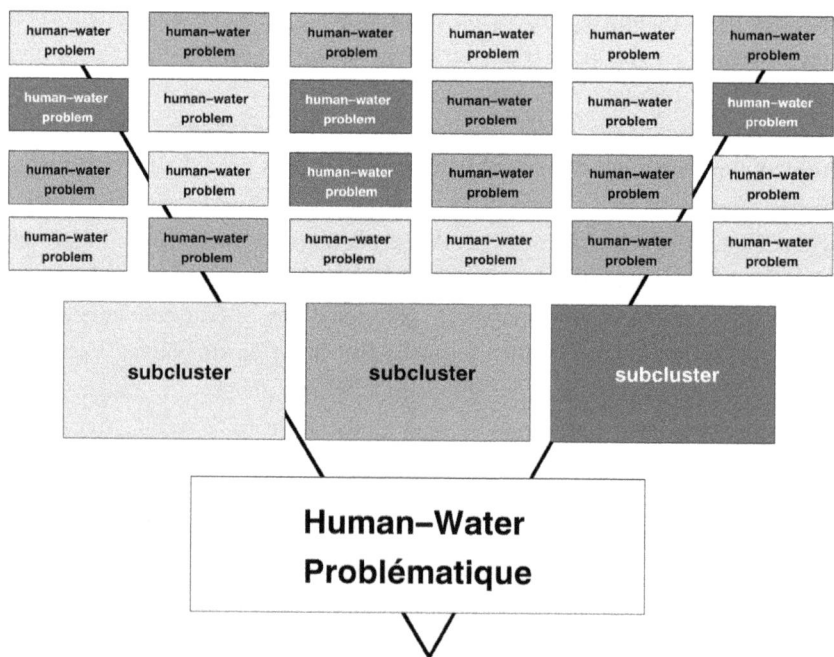

Figure 3 Composition of a problématique, featuring its subcomponents.

Through this process we developed a taxonomy of human–water problématiques (see Figure 4), which we believe characterizes well and gives meaning to the notion of the 'global water crisis.'

All 356 papers at the basis of the taxonomy were coded for location (see Appendix C), and every study focusing on specific countries was synthesized (see Figure 5). This geographic overview is by no means a spatial representation of the importance of different problématiques for each country, it is rather a transparent representation of the geographic focus of the academic literature resulting from the conducted SLR. Nevertheless, it is crucial to critically reflect on the given image. The prevalence of some countries in Figure 5 is relatively well-aligned with the global 'scientific leaders' – i.e., countries generating the largest share of

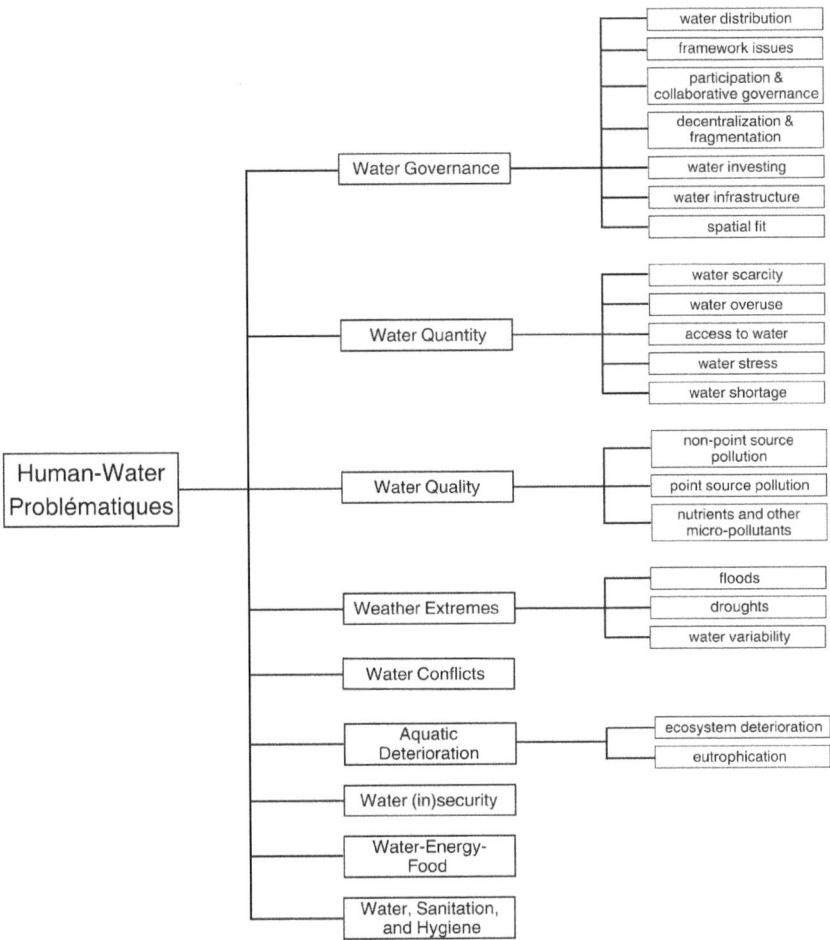

Figure 4 Taxonomy of human–water problématiques.

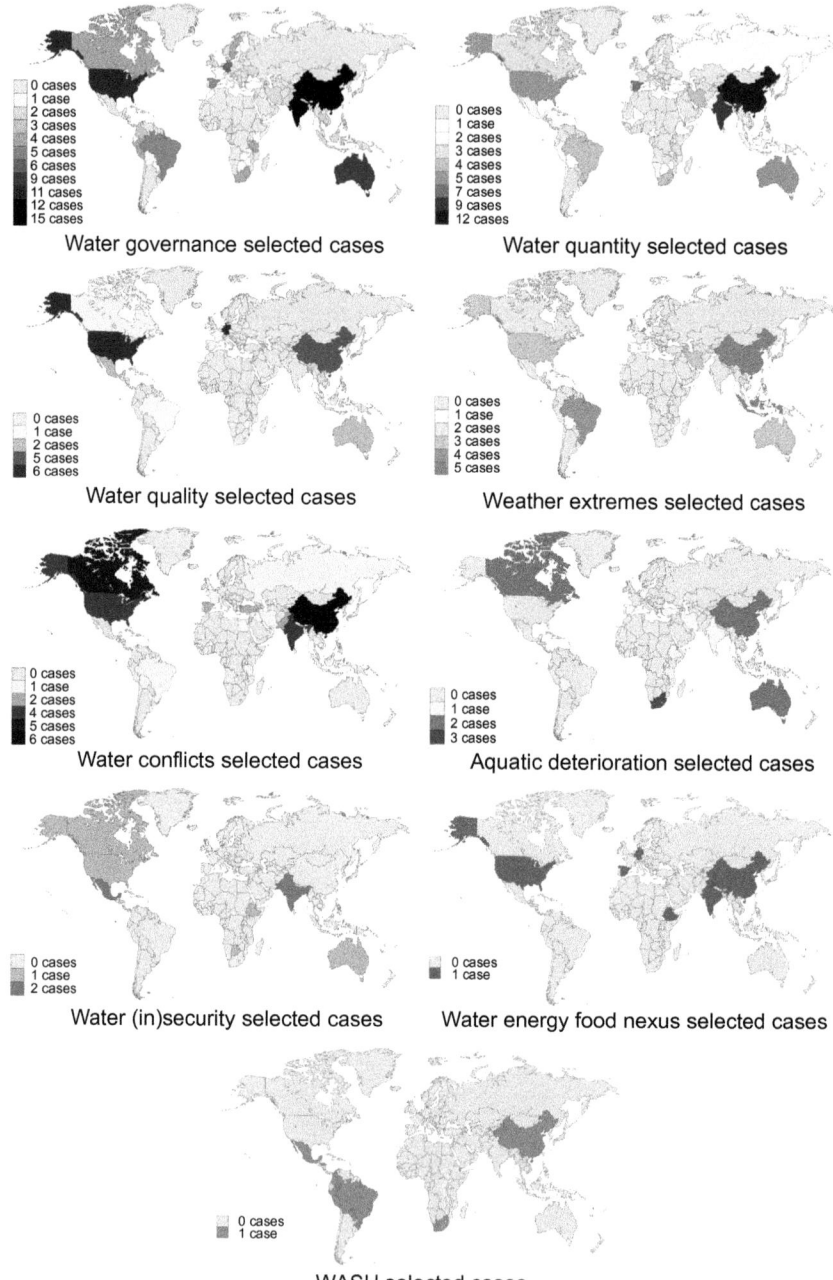

Figure 5 Geographic overview of cases discussed per each problématique.

research output (Nature Index, 2024). These include China, USA, Germany, India, and Australia, as mirrored in the quantified representation of cases per problématique in Appendix C.

There are two points to raise in relation to this alignment. On the one hand, there is the difference between a country being the knowledge producer and a given country being merely used as a case study in work conducted by researchers based at foreign institutes. A temporal analysis by Amarante et al. (2022) concludes in a concerning picture, where the vast majority of research within the field of development is produced by scientists based in the Global North (89 percent over the period of 1990–2019). Similarly, papers where countries and/or regions in the Global South are the focus remain dominated by Northern research (62 percent over the period of 1990–2019). This disparity is further echoed by other authors whose analysis of other fields lead to similar findings (e.g., Bai, 2018; Maas et al., 2021; North, Hastie, & Hoyer, 2020). One consequence of this imbalance is the risk of neglecting local expertise and the nuance of a given context (Amarante et al., 2022; Bai, 2018). Borrowing from Miranda and Zaman (2010), another ramification could be the paradigmatic divergence between the researcher and the case study with which they choose to work. This could result in a potential lack of recognition for context-specific human–water issues at the expense of studying problems that the researchers are familiar with in the context of the Global North. Thus, the prevalence of certain challenges does not directly translate into the given challenge being the most commonly encountered in reality.

On the other hand, strongly linked to the previous point, is the recognition of the bias toward research coming from specific contexts, particularly the resource-wealthy countries such as aforementioned Germany, USA, China, and Australia (Gomez, Herman, & Parigi, 2022). The continuous presence of such countries in global rankings has been linked to research funding and similar support, as well as the institutional architecture and the national scientific infrastructure encountered by local researchers (Amarante et al., 2022; Aydin et al., 2023; North, Hastie, & Hoyer, 2020). However, there is a growing acknowledgment of citation bias toward research produced by scientists based in the Global North or similar resource-wealthy countries (Gomez, Herman, & Parigi, 2022; Nielsen & Andersen, 2021). Despite the steadily growing knowledge production in the Global South, the scholarship does not translate into high citation counts and recognition (Collyer, 2018). This underrepresentation poses a major threat to innovative knowledge circulation, while risking invisibilization of voices and worldviews that fall outside the dominant paradigm (Gomez, Herman, & Parigi, 2022; Rojas & Postigo, 2025). However, an extensive exploration of this matter falls beyond the scope of this research.

3.1 A Global Water Crisis Glossary

This glossary illustrates each problématique and their human–water problem subcomponents. Each explanation is based on five prominent sources retrieved from both our problématiques database and a targeted search. The aim of this glossary is to provide concrete meaning to the the often-ambiguous umbrella term of global water crisis. We show that the global water crisis, from an analytical point of view, is much more complex than assumed and generally depicted. Despite the context-dependence and complexity of each of the identified human–water problems, this Element pinpoints nine key human–water problématiques. 'Water governance' appear as the most common problématique, followed by 'water quantity', 'water quality', 'weather extremes', 'water conflicts', 'aquatic deterioration', 'water (in)security', 'water–energy–food nexus,' and 'water, sanitation, and hygiene' (see Figure 4). It is worth mentioning that, following the definition of a problématique offered at the start of this Element, this Element excluded publications that discuss marine water problems. Thus, issues such as sea-level rise or sea water intrusion have fallen beyond the scope of this research.

3.1.1 Water Governance

Reviewing 'water governance' as an academic field or domain of action is beyond the scope of this description. Following our methodology, we here characterize 'water governance' as a problématique that is defined by seven different clusters of human–water problems that emerge in the academic literature: (1) water distribution; (2) participation and collaborative governance; (3) decentralization and fragmentation; (4) framework issues; (5) water infrastructure; (6) water investing; and (7) spatial fit.

3.1.1.1 Water Distribution

In the context of increasing water stress and competition between water uses, there is a need for water governance practices that allocate water in an efficient manner, balancing supply and demand (Goetz, Martínez, & Xabadia, 2017). At the same time, many authors (e.g., Calzada, Iranzo, & Sanz, 2017; Jackson & Barber, 2013) emphasize the need to prioritize equity matters, assigning distributional justice a more central role in the context of water allocation decision-making (Goetz, Martínez, & Xabadia, 2017). Due to its status as a basic utility, water provision is normally guaranteed by the state (Calzada, Iranzo, & Sanz, 2017). However, in some contexts, this conventional model of distribution can be challenged, considering issues such as the limited outreach of formal water deliveries in the majority of cities in the Global South, reaching only 40–70 percent of the local population

(Ahlers et al., 2014). In this context, the literature on water distribution offers two prominent avenues of research. While some authors (e.g., Ahlers et al., 2014; Calzada, Iranzo, & Sanz, 2017) discussing water service provision center their research on informal utilities, others (e.g., Garrick et al., 2009; Goetz, Martínez, & Xabadia, 2017) bring in the notion of water markets as a mechanism for water allocation. Going further, water provision is normally discussed through an instrumental lens (Alhers et al., 2014). However, these authors underscore the importance of water values that go beyond the conventional material functionality of water, emphasizing the cultural, symbolic, and spiritual dimensions. This nuanced focus is mirrored by other academics, such as Jackson and Barber (2013), who argue for the accommodation of such values in water allocation planning processes, particularly in the context of Indigenous peoples.

3.1.1.2 Participation and Collaborative Governance

In the recent decades, water management and governance has been experiencing a "major paradigm shift" (Pahl-Wostl et al., 2007, p. 5). The reliance on technical experts has given way to practices of collaborative governance. Collaborative governance is a multi-actor decision-making process, where diverse stakeholders engage across the boundaries of different levels and spheres, such as the public–private dichotomy, to address a public purpose together, as individual approaches are deemed inadequate (Cuadrado-Quesada & Schwartz, 2022; Dewulf et al., 2011). In consequence, coalitions between government institutions and various politically unconventional actors, such as local communities, have become a point of interest in the domain of water governance (Cuadrado-Quesada & Schwartz, 2022; Dewulf et al., 2011).

Many authors (e.g., Cuadrado-Quesada & Schwartz, 2022; Heyd & Neef, 2006; Imperial, 2005) highlight the preference for collaborative practices in the domain of water governance due to the efficiency, sustainability, and effectiveness of such approaches to water management queries. Accordingly, Heyd and Neef (2006) show evidence on higher success rates of participatory watershed projects, in comparison to "externally managed, top-down, 'one-size-fits-all' projects" (p. 398), pointing toward a record of top-down water project failures in South and East Asia. Nevertheless, Imperial (2005) emphasizes that collaborative governance should not be seen as a silver bullet solution, and ought to instead be used by policymakers with caution. What is more, collaborative approaches can face significant challenges. Cuadrado-Quesada and Schwartz (2022) explore the failed governance process in the Netherlands, where most of the initially involved actors decided to exit the collaboration due to the stark contrasts in their understanding of the problem on hand, resulting in financially burdening the stakeholders who remained. The challenge of conflicting framing is echoed by Dewulf et al. (2011), who illustrate that the process of framing the scale of a problem leads to delineating which problems and actors are to be considered.

3.1.1.3 Decentralization and Fragmentation

Decentralization implies the existence of multiple independent centers of authority (Pahl-Wostl & Knieper, 2014). Applied to water governance, this means that water issues are governed locally by a set of actors, as opposed to a single general ruler. Decentralization in water governance derives from the concept of subsidiarity (Pahl-Wostl, Gupta, & Petry, 2008; Pahl-Wostl & Knieper, 2014). The principle of subsidiarity states that environmental or social issues should be addressed by the most local institution with the competence to solve that issue, while higher-level institutions should at most support the action of the local institution. Typically, water governance happens on different levels, from local, to national, basin, and global levels (Pahl-Wostl, Gupta, & Petry, 2008).

Decentralization in water governance has gained popularity in the last decades because of its supposed ability to address wicked problems generated by climate change and other global changes (Pahl-Wostl & Knieper, 2014). In fact, splitting the role of who should take care of extremely complex problems among different actors, instead of attributing it to a single, despite articulated, governing structure, allows simultaneously to split the otherwise unmanageably complex challenge into simpler, more solvable, problems or problem components (Edelenbos & Teisman, 2011). Historically, water governance was a strongly hierarchical process until the 1950s–1960s, when the subsidiarity principle gained popularity (Pahl-Wostl & Knieper, 2014). This initially led to a market-based decentralization, until the emergence of participatory approaches at the end of the twentieth century made it clear that communities should be at the center of decentralized water governance structures (Pahl-Wostl & Knieper, 2014).

While, as of today, the advantages of decentralized water governance are broadly acknowledged, their functioning relies on a condition that is often overlooked. Indeed, as it had been already highlighted by Elinor and Vincent Ostrom, functioning decentralized water governance systems implicitly require that the distinct, independent centers of authority all follow a single, shared, overarching set of rules (Pahl-Wostl & Knieper, 2014, p. 140). This is also essentially the difference between decentralization and fragmentation. Both terminologies define governance systems that rely on a set of institutions instead of concentrating power in the hands of a single actor, but, while decentralized systems are, indeed, systems, in the sense that they have a degree of coordination given by a set of common rules, fragmentation is a problem of uncoordinated plural governance systems (Edelenbos & Teisman, 2011; Pahl-Wostl & Knieper, 2014). When the absence of coordination transforms decentralized systems into fragmented ones, the ability to decompose and solve wicked problems transforms into an accountability shifting phenomenon, where responsibility for action is continuously passed from one actor the another, ultimately hindering the capacity to solve the problem (Edelenbos & Teisman, 2011).

Complex problems remain unsolvable if their components are addressed separately in a fragmented way, instead of keeping an integrated approach given by coordination among authority centers. Another issue could be a mismatch between levels on which water governance is implemented, where different levels work in contrast with each other (Pahl-Wostl, Gupta, & Petry, 2008). Indeed, experimental approaches have shown that there is a need for a coordinated mix of decentralized and centralized structures, often, but not always, corresponding to informal and formal water governance approaches, respectively (Rijke et al., 2013). Moreover, in the light of global challenges, it has become evident that, beyond the co-presence of different levels of centralization–decentralization (e.g., water governance at local–national–watershed–global level), research on the interactions between those levels is needed, so that multilevel water governance structures can be developed (Pahl-Wostl, Gupta, & Petry, 2008). The expectation here, although with a sensible degree of uncertainty, is that local water governance structures, located closer to where the impacts of global challenges happen, can motivate and drive to action global actors, which have the capacity to address these challenges in an integrated way (Pahl-Wostl, Gupta, & Petry, 2008).

3.1.1.4 Framework Issues

In the field of water management, the concept of 'framework issues' refers to the challenges encountered in implementing effective strategies to ensure the sustainable use and conservation of water resources. Several articles shed light on these issues, mainly within the context of integrated water resources management (IWRM) and the Water Framework Directive (WFD), providing valuable insights into the complexities of managing water sustainably.

One of the significant challenges identified in implementing the WFD is the need for improved coordination among various sectors and stakeholders. As highlighted in Voulvoulis, Arpon, and Giakoumis (2017), the integration of different water-related sectors has proven to be a complex task. Achieving coherence among sectors such as agriculture, industry, and urban planning requires effective collaboration and coordination to ensure holistic water management practices. Additionally, stakeholder engagement plays a crucial role in addressing framework issues. Zingraff-Hamed et al. (2020) emphasize the importance of involving diverse stakeholders in decision-making processes. Inconsistent interpretation and application of the WFD requirements, limited financial resources, and insufficient stakeholder engagement have been identified as bottlenecks in effectively implementing the directive. Bridging the gap between policy and practice necessitates active participation and collaboration among stakeholders at all levels. Moreover, the success of framework implementation relies on monitoring and assessment mechanisms. Hering et al. (2010) evaluate the achievements and shortcomings of the WFD over a decade, emphasizing the importance of refining ecological assessment methods and enhancing the integration of socioeconomic aspects within monitoring and assessment frameworks. Strengthening governance structures and improving the effectiveness of water management practices are recommended for the future.

A more comprehensive approach to water management is advocated through the concept of IWRM. This emphasizes the integration of ecological, social, and economic considerations (Biswas, 2004). However, challenges in achieving effective IWRM have been identified. This, similarly, includes coordination among various sectors, integrating socioeconomic aspects into water management plans, and implementing adaptive management strategies to address uncertainties (Medema McIntosh, & Jeffrey, 2008).

Framework issues in water management, therefore, encompass challenges related to coordination among sectors and stakeholders, stakeholder engagement, integration of socioeconomic aspects, and monitoring and assessment mechanisms. These challenges must be addressed to achieve sustainable water management practices. By considering insights from various articles, policymakers and water managers can work toward overcoming these framework issues, ensuring the efficient and sustainable use of water resources for the benefit of present and future generations.

3.1.1.5 Water Infrastructure

Infrastructures in the water governance sector often play a double role as both part of problems and of solutions. Water infrastructures include those for water provision and sanitation, especially in urban and peri-urban areas, as well as irrigation, storage, and drainage infrastructures (Khan, Hanjra, & Mu, 2009;

Silveti & Andersson, 2019). One of the main challenges associated with infrastructures is the inability of infrastructure development to keep up with trends in infrastructure demand. One instance is the slower rate of development of infrastructure in peri-urban areas with respect to the population increase in peri-urban areas themselves, especially in the case of sanitation infrastructures (Silveti & Andersson, 2019).

Indeed, infrastructure investment is one of the major development challenges for megacities, assuming different forms (e.g., investments for renovation or setup) depending on the level of development and on the local history of infrastructure development. These challenges are associated not only with the growth rate of urban and peri-urban population, but clearly also to the rate of geographic growth of megacities, and their overall extension (Li, Endter-Wada, & Li, 2015). Although in some cases it is virtually impossible to avoid it, this mismatch between infrastructure supply and demand can lead to environmental damage, as local water dwellers adapt by relying on more unsustainable alternative water infrastructure solutions. This can ultimately lead to slowing down the urban expansion and development process itself (Srinivasan et al., 2013).

The challenge of infrastructure development relates also to the challenge of food security. This is less related to water sanitation infrastructures and more to irrigation infrastructures, with irrigation expansion as one of the proposed solutions for increasing agricultural production, and thus food security, not without environmental impacts (Khan, Hanjra, & Mu, 2009). Indeed, infrastructure planning and development, together with institutional capacity development and financial solutions, are required to work synergically to achieve sustainable and resilient water systems (Srinivasan et al., 2013). Yet, the planning of water infrastructures is typically predominantly technical, with social science research mostly focused on local willingness to pay for infrastructures or on developmental issues in the Global South (Lienert, Schnetzer, & Ingold, 2013). The focus of engineering solutions is to bring water to more people. This clearly brings intended benefits, however, when not integrated in the planning process, it can also be a limited approach due to the tendency of conflicts to arise around 'new' water supplies (Li, Ng, & Skitmore, 2013). Risks in infrastructure planning also arise when trying to export technological solutions from one context to another (Li, Ng, & Skitmore, 2013). Even though water issues are known to be local and context-specific, water infrastructure planning is usually characterized by lower levels of participation than other planning processes (Lienert, Schnetzer, & Ingold, 2013). This can lead to failures in the application of infrastructures, because they are not well fit to the local context. Additionally, there are issues of low cultural acceptance in regard to nontraditional solutions, even when they provide evident benefits with respect to more culturally and socially rooted types of infrastructure (Silveti & Andersson, 2019).

3.1.1.6 Water Investing

Closely linked to the issue of infrastructure development is the notion of water investing. The value of the global water industry is believed to reach USD700 billion, with Asian countries, in particular China and Japan, Europe, and North America listed as the biggest markets (Roca & Anand Tularam, 2012). An estimate of Roca and Anand Tularam (2012) suggest a need for an investment of up to USD600 billion to the global water industry to effectively address the expected shortages in the global water supply. Simultaneously, the need for stable and water-focused funding has been deemed crucial for the implementation of effective stormwater management programs (Zhao, Fonseca, & Zeerak, 2019).

Goldman-Benner et al. (2012) bring in the concept of water funds, which the authors define as "payment for watershed service project" (p. 56) with a focus on long-term conservation. These initiatives serve as an example of investments in what is referred to as 'natural infrastructure' (Bremer et al., 2016), where downstream users get to fund upstream stewardship through institutional mechanisms (Goldman-Benner et al., 2012). Water funds have experienced a significant proliferation in Latin America. Against the silver bullet approach, each investment project reflects the location-dependent qualities and goals (Bremer et al., 2016; Goldman-Benner et al., 2012). Water funds have been proved a sustainable, long-term investment model for financing conservation (Goldman-Benner et al., 2012).

3.1.1.7 Spatial Fit

Famously defined by Moss (2012) as the "congruence between the geographical extent of a biophysical system and the management area of an institution" (p. 2), spatial fit has become a central point of interest for political and natural resource scientists, geographers, economists, and policymakers (Lee & Moss, 2014). Spatial fit has been listed as the key element responsible for increasing the resilience of a social-ecological system (Herrfahrdt-Pähle, 2014). Problems of spatial fit, understood as institutional failures to account for "nature, functionality, and dynamics of the specific ecosystem" (Moss, 2012, p. 2) given institution influences, are often deemed the central drivers of unsustainable water management (Lee & Moss, 2014). These arise as a result of a mismatch between jurisdictional and ecosystem boundaries, where an institution might cover only a part of a catchment, therefore neglecting and, in some cases, negatively impacting resources outside its jurisdictional scope (Herrfahrdt-Pähle, 2014; Lee & Moss, 2014; Qiu et al., 2017). Examples of such spatial misfit between institutional and ecosystem boundaries include resource overuse of pollution, diminishing the adaptive capacity and resilience of a given system (Herrfahrdt-Pähle, 2014; Moss, 2012).

There is an agreement amongst scholars that striving to achieve a 'perfect spatial fit' is a futile task (del Moral & Do Ó, 2014; Herrfahrdt-Pähle, 2014; Lee & Moss, 2014; Moss, 2012). Since the 1980s, there has been a growing recognition of shortcomings of perceiving spatial fit as a panacea (Moss, 2012). Treating spatial fit as a "normative category for institutional design" (Moss, 2012, p. 9) poses significant challenges due to the inherent difficulty of delineating territorial boundaries of a shifting resource and due to the risk of neglecting the socio-political, cultural, and economic dimensions of the given ecosystem or resource. Indeed, another area of agreement concerns the need to move beyond the strictly spatial understanding of the concept. Many authors (e.g., del Moral & Do Ó, 2014; Lee & Moss, 2014; Qiu et al., 2017) call for an acknowledgment of the power dynamics and constellations underlying the decision-making processes related to the concept of spatial fit.

Instead of a panacea, spatial fit ought to be seen as an "analytical frame for revealing the multiple geographies of resource management, the problems that these may generate, and the options for addressing them" (del Moral & Do Ó, 2014, p. 343). In a similar vein, this nuanced understanding of the concept paves a way for seeing and applying spatial fit as a practice of adaptive (co-) management, with an array of actors across diverse scales and spatial context (Moss, 2012).

3.1.2 Water Quantity

Water quantity, as well, is a problématique composed by different subclusters. Different human–water problems, related to scarcity, overuse, access, stress, and shortages characterize this domain.

3.1.2.1 Water Scarcity

As argued by some authors (see Graffy, 2006; Rijsberman, 2006), there is no universally agreed-upon definition of water scarcity. The term can be understood in a number of ways, some more technical than others. One of the most commonly referred to conceptions of scarcity in the media is the relationship between water availability and freshwater demand, in particular in terms of water available per capita annually (Mekonnen & Hoekstra, 2016; Rijsberman,

2006). Scarcity occurs when many people in a given area are water insecure – that is, without access to satisfactory water resources, for an extended period of time. Indeed, this mismatch is what lies at the heart of water scarcity, making it a broad term that can be further distinguished into stress and shortage (Mekonnen & Hoekstra, 2016).

A more technical definition could be the relationship between blue water footprint and total blue water availability (Mekonnen & Hoekstra, 2016). Relying on the Falkenmark indicator, widely used to represent water scarcity, but also water shortage and stress, an annual supply of less than 1,000 m^3 of renewable resources per capita displays water scarcity, while a supply falling short of 500 m^3 indicates absolute scarcity. Simultaneously, the plethora of perspectives and definitions results in the portrayal of water scarcity as an issue of shortages (insufficient water resources), sanitation (insufficient clean resources), or governance (insufficient well-allocated resources) (Graffy, 2006).

Depending on the definition, one's understanding of water scarcity can be molded by factors such as how one's needs are defined or whether water resources in a given location are made fully or only partially available for use (Rijsberman, 2006). With this in mind, a distinction can be made between economic water scarcity and physical water scarcity. The former refers to a condition where, despite the abundance of the resource economic and/or institutional capability, is insufficient to make water available for human use. In this sense, it poses a supply problem. The latter is seen in the cases of so-called thirsty cities, where water running out due to demand exceeding available resources is a reality, constituting a demand problem and what in turn becomes water stress, as explained later (Molle & Berkoff, 2009; Rijsberman, 2006). Eneng, Lulofs, and Asdak (2018) complete the list by adding relative scarcity, which they define as a situation where, due to unequal access, some actors receive less water than others despite the overall abundance of the resource.

As emphasized by Mekonnen and Hoekstra (2016), accurate water scarcity assessment ought to include the fluctuations across seasons in terms of water consumed and water available. Thus, scarcity is time-bound. The authors revealed that, at the time of writing, 4 billion people were shown to face severe water scarcity for at least 1 month per year, out of which, almost half were located in India and China. Half a billion of the global population live under conditions of severe water scarcity throughout the year.

3.1.2.2 Water Overuse

Despite the existence of several interpretations, overexploitation can simply refer to an intensive use of a water resource, which in consequence poses a threat to the long-term quantity and quality preservation, as well as to the related ecosystem services (Leduc, Pulido-Bosch, & Remini, 2017). As reported by Wada and Bierkens (2014), such unsustainable consumption of water resources has been on the rise, particularly since the late 1990s, with mentions of surface- and groundwater resource overuse being increasingly present in water research.

When discussing water overexploitation, many authors (e.g., Holley & Sinclair, 2013; Leduc, Pulido-Bosch, & Remini, 2017; Shankar, Kulkarni, & Krishnan, 2011; Wada et al., 2010) choose to focus on groundwater resources. Groundwater took center stage only in the past few decades (Shankar, Kulkarni, & Krishnan, 2011). This could be linked to the growing human reliance on nonrenewable groundwater resources globally, which have become the "obvious choice to fill a gap between the increasing demand and limited availability of surface freshwater" (Wada & Bierkens, 2014, p. 12).

In this context, overexploitation occurs when the rate of groundwater abstraction "exceeds the natural groundwater recharge for extensive areas and long times" (Wada et al., 2010, p. 1). Irrigation, particularly for agricultural purposes, has been listed as the leading driver of groundwater exploitation (Wada et al., 2010). Historically, this trend has been particularly visible over (semi-)arid regions, such as in the Middle East and North Africa and the Mediterranean regions (Leduc, Pulido-Bosch, & Remini, 2017; Wada & Bierkens, 2014). Nevertheless, the consequences of unsustainable water use go beyond the specific region, often occurring on a global scale (Wada & Bierkens, 2014).

Leduc, Pulido-Bosch, and Remini (2017) emphasize the issue of data scarcity for global aquifers, limiting the effectiveness of present and future governance of groundwater resources. Limited information availability decreases the accuracy of vulnerability assessment. Similarly, groundwater exploitation assessments can yield significant discrepancies in their estimates. One reason for this could be the rare consideration of nonrenewable resource use in water indicators (Wada & Bierkens, 2014). Another issue relates to the seeming lack of urgency in regard to groundwater governance on a policy level (Shankar, Kulkarni, & Krishnan, 2011). This might have to do with the fact that in many countries, with India serving as the most prominent example, extreme overexploitation "coexists with relatively low levels of extraction" (p. 39) across the country.

Several measures could be undertaken to avert the ongoing trends, such as improved water recycling and irrigation schemes, dietary change and reforms to the current mechanisms of water management, and governance, including the introduction of relevant economic incentives (Holley & Sinclair, 2013; Wada & Bierkens, 2014).

3.1.2.3 Access to Water

By the end of the MDGs era, an estimate of those with no access to water remained at 663 million, resulting in an unmet target on improved sanitation (Hove et al., 2019). According to the dominant ('wide') view, access to water is understood as coverage. Obeng-Odoom (2012) calls for a distinction between this wide view and what he refers to as deep access – concerning "affordability, quality, distribution, and reliability" (p. 1135) of water resources. Issues with access to water, understood both through the lens of the dominant and the deep view, prevail mainly in developing countries (Moe & Rheingans, 2006; Vásquez & Franceschi, 2013).

Such an understanding puts statements of increased water access in question. A transition to a deep understanding of access to water in international development discourse is needed to accurately depict people's experiences in accessing water in practice, taking into consideration wider social consequences (Obeng-Odoom, 2012). Simultaneously, applying a deep understanding of water access allows us to move away from perceiving water as an economic good in favor of seeing it as a right (Obeng-Odoom, 2012).

Hove et al. (2019) offer an extensive list of health and societal costs, emphasizing the diverse dimensions of access to water. For instance, a relationship between access to water and poverty has been suggested by several studies on the Global South (Hove et al., 2019; Moe & Rheingans, 2006; Toure et al., 2012). Inequitable access to water has been linked to disparities in resource availability, but also "income, power, and institutional capacity between and within countries" (Moe & Rheingans, 2006, p. 51). Similarly, Toure et al. (2012) emphasize the correlation between access to water and urban dynamics (growing population and swelling water demand). Some case studies (e.g., Vásquez & Franceschi, 2013) discuss the relationship between the demand for improved reliability of water services and age, showing that "willingness to pay for improved water services seems to decrease with age" (p. 4922). In a similar vein, poor access is believed to disproportionately impact women and children (Moe & Rheingans, 2006).

Hove et al. (2019) link water access to effective governance structures. At the same time, the transformative potential of community participation in facilitating the process through highlighting and resolving access issues is increasingly recognized (Moe & Rheingans, 2006; Vásquez & Franceschi, 2013).

3.1.2.4 Water Shortage

Falling under the umbrella of 'physical water scarcity,' water shortage represents population-driven scarcity, positioned next to demand-driven scarcity, which in turn is understood as 'water stress' (Kummu et al., 2010). Water shortage considers the number of people between whom a unit of water is divided, offering a specific freshwater availability per capita. Key contributors are the growing population and variability in the hydrologic cycle due to climate change (Kummu et al., 2010; Pimentel et al., 2004). However, as stressed by Webber et al. (2015), "different cities face water shortages for different reasons" (p. 407); hence, each case requires a context-specific analysis.

Following the typology proposed by Kummu et al. (2010), a distinction can be made between moderate water shortage and chronic water shortage. While the former refers to a threshold of available resources of 1,000–1,700 m^3 per capita annually, as determined by the Falkenmark indicator, the latter is used in cases of availability falling below 1,000 m^3 per capita annually. The authors make a further differentiation between high (500–1,000 m^3/person/year) and extreme (less than 500 m^3/person/year) water shortage. Water shortages can also be understood in terms of water runoff rate (Pimentel et al., 2004).

Trends in global water shortages have been linked with other water-related phenomena, including a significant geographical overlap between water shortages and heightened groundwater abstraction (Kummu et al., 2010). Simultaneously, water shortage has been discussed in the context of food security, as "water availability and accessibility are the most significant constraining factors for crop production" (Mancosu et al., 2015, p. 976). Pimentel et al. (2004) add the linkage between water shortage and ecosystem degradation, with signs of severe aquatic and terrestrial biodiversity loss.

Historically, the key focus in solving the issue of water shortage has been the increase of water availability through, for example, abstraction of groundwater resources, dam constructions, or inter-basin water transfers (Gohari et al., 2013; Kummu et al., 2010; Webber et al., 2015). However, such measures have been proven to be insufficient in some regions; thus, suggesting a transition toward 'soft' non-structural measures centered around increased water use efficiency and similar socioeconomic reforms (Gohari et al., 2013; Kummu et al., 2010; Mancosu et al., 2015; Pimentel et al., 2004). Similarly, many authors (e.g., Mancosu et al., 2015) emphasize the pivotal role of virtual water as a driver or compensation in water short areas.

3.1.2.5 Water Stress

Understood as demand-driven scarcity, water stress refers to the level of pressure imposed on water resources and ecosystems by external factors, the main one being increasing water withdrawals. The higher the water withdrawal, the higher the degradation and/or exhaustion, resulting in increased water stress levels (Alcamo, Flörke, & Märker, 2007). Simultaneously, water stress is linked to the uneven distributions of freshwater, both in space and in time, and to the heightened competition between diverse users and uses, as well as regional insecurity (Alcamo, Flörke, & Märker, 2007; Oki & Kanae, 2006; Richey et al., 2015).

There are several ways of assessing water stress, the main ones being: (1) resource availability measured per capita; (2) ratio or difference between water use and resource availability; and (3) the assessment of physical and socioeconomic aspects influencing stress levels (Arnell, 2004; Richey et al., 2015). However, Alcamo, Flörke, and Märker (2007) voice concern of using "aggregated indicators to describe the complex processes of water stress" (p. 250), suggesting a preference for a comparison between the scores of diverse indicators. Moreover, some authors (e.g., Alcamo, Flörke, & Märker, 2007; Arnell, 2004; Richey et al., 2015) point to the disparities in the specification of thresholds when defining who is affected by water stress. McDonald et al. (2014) highlight the need to recognize the role of urban water infrastructure in accurate estimations of population living under water stress, as many stressed cities import water from a "cumulative distance of 27,000 ± 3800 km" (p. 103). Despite such shortcomings and the risk of oversimplification, indicators remain useful as a benchmark facilitating the assessment of the global state of water stress (Alcamo, Flörke, & Märker, 2007).

A specific numeric score is brought in by Arnell (2004), who defines water-stressed watersheds as those with runoff lower than 1,000 m^3 per capita per year. The widely used Falkenmark indicator states that an amount falling between 1,000 m^3 and 1,700 m^3 per capita per year signifies moderate stress, a threshold of 500–1,000 m^3 per capita per year indicates high stress, while amounts below this line fall in the extreme stress category (Arnell, 2004). The UN Renewable Stress Scale relies on the stress ratio (water use to resource availability), dividing potential stress levels into low, moderate, high, and extreme (score of higher than 0.4) (Richey et al., 2015). Similarly, applying the water scarcity index, calculated as the difference between annual water withdrawals by all sectors and the water use from desalinated water, further divided by the annual available renewable freshwater resources, a score higher than 0.4 indicates high water stress (Oki & Kanae, 2006). Richey et al. (2015) suggest a spectrum of stress regime behaviors based on the estimated outcome of use and annual recharge of water resources. These can be classified into unstressed, variable stress, human-dominated variable stress, and overstressed.

With an increasing dependence on groundwater resources, some authors (e.g., McDonald et al., 2014; Richey et al., 2015) offer surface- and groundwater-specific water stress indicators. This is due to the fact that many most commonly used indicators, such as the Falkenmark indicator, do not account for groundwater. Renewable groundwater stress can be defined as the "ratio of groundwater use to groundwater availability" (Richey et al., 2015, p. 5218). Groundwater stress is linked to a number of negative consequences, ranging from land subsistence to ecosystem destruction (Richey et al., 2015).

Despite the existence of several indicators and their disparities when defining thresholds, a certain geographic overlap can be derived when it comes to global water-stressed areas. These include predominantly semiarid to arid regions, including the Middle East, northern and southern Africa, central Mexico, southwestern USA, northeast Brazil, and western parts of South America (Alcamo, Flörke, & Märker, 2007; Richey at al., 2015).

3.1.3 Water Quality

The scientific discussion on water quality is mainly concentrated around 'nonpoint source (NPS) pollutants.' Some authors make a distinction in the type of the NPS pollutant, resulting in the identification of three subclusters: (1) nonspecified NPS pollution; (2) nutrients and other NPS micro-pollutants; and (3) point-source (PS) pollution.

3.1.3.1 NPS Pollution

The term nonpoint source pollutants refers to substances that originate from human activities but whose source is difficult to discern (Short, 2013). Their roots are numerous and diffused throughout a catchment, making governance of NPS pollution particularly challenging (Patterson, 2016; Patterson, Smith, & Bellamy, 2015; Sun et al., 2012). Some of the most commonly encountered NPS pollutants are nutrients, sediments, and toxicants of, for example, pharmaceutical origin (Patterson, 2016; Short, 2013).

The problem of NPS pollution is not exclusive to surface water. The issue of groundwater pollution from diffuse sources has been gaining attention in water governance literature, with nitrates listed as one of the leading pollutants (Kirschke, Borchardt, & Newig, 2017; Sun et al., 2012).

Nonpoint source pollution is increasingly recognized as one of the leading impairments to water quality globally, with the management of this issue deemed "critical to maintaining water quality and availability, ecosystem services, and human wellbeing" (Patterson, Smith, & Bellamy, 2015, p. 480). Nonetheless, effective NPS pollution control remains a challenge, as the issue is a case of a 'wicked problem' – that is, a complex problem resistant to conventional interventions, involving a plethora of actors, drivers, and scales (Kirschke, Borchardt, & Newig, 2017; Patterson, 2015).

Effective management of NPS pollution is dependent on collective action in a multi-scalar context (Patterson, 2015). Examples of initiatives to address the issue include the European Union's (EU's) WFD or the Clean Water Act in USA; however, NPS pollution remains a persistent problem.

3.1.3.2 Nutrients and Other Micro-pollutants

Taking a closer look at publications obtained through the SLR discussing water quality, some sources specify the type of NPS pollutant they are dealing with. In such cases, the focus tends to fall predominantly on nutrient pollution. A growing body of literature is attempting to address the problem of both surface- and groundwater nutrient pollution, mainly that of nitrogen from agricultural sources (i.e., fertilizers) (e.g., Kirschke et al., 2019; Sixt et al., 2019). Nitrogen has been heavily relied upon by farmers globally to intensify agricultural production, entering water reserves and ecosystems through water runoff (Kirschke et al., 2019). As pointed out in the study on Nebraska's groundwater governance, nitrates are "the most common chemical contaminant in groundwater worldwide" (Sixt et al., 2019, p. 676).

Nutrient pollution is one of the central focuses of the EU's WFD, yet its wicked nature poses a major challenge for policymakers across the EU countries (Wiering et al., 2020). The difficulty stems partially from the nexus dimension of the problem, where interests of diverse stakeholders are at play, and the fragmentation of the institutional landscape, where the lack of linkages between water and agriculture are particularly hindering (Kirschke et al., 2019). As noted by Sixt et al. (2019), solutions to nitrates pollution ought to be context specific. This is echoed by other researchers who move beyond panacean prescriptions to acknowledge local culture, political structure, and other institutional aspects (Wiering et al., 2020). Another element deemed effective is collaboration between diverse actors, integrated approaches, and polycentric distribution of decision-making (Kirschke et al., 2019; Sixt et al., 2019; Wiering et al., 2020).

Two additional trends were detected when coding publications within the water quality problématique. Microplastics and heavy metals (such as lead, arsenic, and copper) are increasingly encountered in water bodies worldwide. This occurrence is linked to increased anthropogenic activity – industrial plants, untreated domestic waste, and agriculture (Islam et al., 2015; Su et al., 2016). In both cases, microplastics and heavy metals were found in aquatic biota, not only water resources. What is more, microplastics have been found in remote water bodies, suggesting a nearly omnipresent existence (Su et al., 2016).

3.1.3.3 PS Pollution

Standing in contrast to NPS pollutants, PS inputs "derive from a localized situation and enter a water body at a specific or restricted number of locations" (Reichenberger et al., 2007, p. 3). Many authors (e.g., Carey & Migliaccio, 2009; Carr, Liu, & Tesoro, 2016; McCormick et al., 2014) list effluent from wastewater treatment plants (WWTPs) as one of the key sources of PS pollutants. Others (e.g., Reichenberger et al., 2007; Wu & Chen, 2013) mention farmland runoff as the main origin, followed by industrial wastewater discharge and accidental spills (industrial or mining-induced).

The PS pollution scholarship appears to center its focus around WWTPs and micropollutants, with microplastics being of particular interest in recent years. The discussion on WWTPs often touches upon the challenges of complete water filtration due to factors such as high costs, alongside limitations of existing infrastructure and associated technology (Carey & Migliaccio, 2009; McCormick et al., 2014; Reichenberger et al., 2007). Within the micropollutant-centered literature on PS pollution, a specific trend could be distinguished. The focus on nutrients and pesticides, which seems to dominate the literature in the early 2000s, appears to be giving way to a growing interest in microplastics, beginning around the mid-2010s onward.

Often, distinguishing NPS and PS pollution can pose a significant challenge (Reichenberger et al., 2007). However, one difference shown by Carey and Migliaccio (2009) is that nutrient pollution has a stronger link to WWTP overflow than to other NPS origins. Yet, in the case of microplastics, Carr, Liu, and Tesoro (2016) argue that WWTP discharge serves only as a minor contributor to aquatic microplastic pollution. In this case, the authors emphasize the difference between microplastic from household uses or commercial products, which are the most encountered types in a treatment plant, and the primary microplastic sources in aquatic ecosystems, which are predominantly derived from consumer packaging.

Literature focusing on solutions to PS pollution does not appear as developed as the scholarship discussing NPS pollution. Key suggestions include awareness campaigns targeting farmers to ensure responsible use of agricultural products and efforts to increase effectiveness of wastewater handling (Reichenberger et al., 2007; Wu & Chen, 2013). Another central point refers back to the often-seen entanglement of NPS and PS pollutants. As argued by Reichenberger et al. (2007), PS pollution ought not to be tackled in isolation from NPS pollution. The focus of the efforts should be of dual nature.

3.1.4 Weather Extremes

Weather extremes can be distinguished in three main subclusters relating to floods, droughts, and a body of literature that discusses the extreme fluctuations of water resources.

3.1.4.1 Floods

Floods are the water extreme with the strongest research record. Indeed, floodplains are a clear example of human–water systems in their most integrated form, as human interventions can significantly alter flood risk (in both directions), and living in an area prone to floods has a strong impact on human activities (di Baldassarre et al., 2013). Including the components of flood hazard, exposed goods, and people, and their vulnerability in the definition of flood risk has translated into a set of established practices at the policy level. These feature flood risk evaluation, alongside mapping, and management through structural and nonstructural measures.

These practices have led to a typical flood governance approach that is largely based on technical expertise, and focused on the prevention of, and active protection from, flood risk (Molenveld & van Buuren, 2019). Yet, climate change is increasing the frequency and intensity of flood events, while other global changes such as urbanization and demographic growth are heightening the exposure and vulnerability to floods (IPCC, 2023; Jiang, Zevenbergen, & Fu, 2017; Molenveld & van Buuren, 2019). Therefore, flood governance approaches based solely on prevention and protection may become less effective, and a paradigm shift is needed towards softer approaches, aiming at increasing the resilience of communities and infrastructure, and their adaptation capacity to a flood risk that is becoming increasingly difficult to reduce (Butler & Pidgeon, 2011; Molenveld & van Buuren, 2019).

The approaches to flood governance further intertwine with how the structure of flood risk management processes is set up, not only to its guiding principles. Traditional flood risk management has a strong prescriptive component, based on technical evaluations of flood risk. Nonetheless, citizen participation is another key component in flood risk management, and, in some legislations, it is even mandatory (Wehn et al., 2015). Enabling citizens to participate in flood risk management processes can be a step toward implementation of innovative policies. Providing citizens with information and technologies that support their involvement in such processes allows them to contribute to better frame policies in a demand-driven sense, and even to innovate the participatory process itself (Wehn et al., 2015).

Evidently, innovative polycentric flood governance approaches often encounter resistance of the main actors in traditional flood governance institutions and structures (Molenveld & van Buuren, 2019). However, participatory flood risk management approaches do not position themselves in a completely alternative space with respect to traditional approaches. Approaches combining the evidence-based component and the participatory component can help create new, unconventional forms of flood risk framing and governance (di Baldassarre et al., 2013).

3.1.4.2 Droughts

Drought is an extreme weather event, driven by climatic variables, during which precipitations over land decrease below what are defined as the 'normal' amounts (Dai, 2011). Since droughts are defined as a relative precipitation decrease with respect to the regular local rainfall conditions, they can occur both in areas with typically high and low rainfall rates. Droughts can last from weeks to several months, thus occurring on a longer timescale than heat waves but on a shorter one than aridity (Dai, 2011; Mishra & Singh, 2010). Many meteo-climatic factors such as heat, high winds, low relative humidity, and timing and intensity of rainfall, as well as the interactions of these factors with agriculture are all relevant factors in the development of drought events (Mishra & Singh, 2010).

Due to its slow onset, diverse drivers, and long lasting and pervasive impacts, diverse definitions of drought have been provided by different actors, often depending on the variable, or the metric considered as representative for drought (Dai, 2011; Mishra & Singh, 2010). The impact propagation chain is complex and multifaceted – it includes impacts on: (1) agriculture, reflecting on food supplies and prices; (2) energy supply and prices, through the lack of cooling water, low hydroelectric storages, and energy crop failures; (3) environment; and (4) municipal and industrial water users (Grigg, 2014).

Global warming has increased the persistence and intensity of droughts as a result of alterations in the atmospheric circulation. This trend is expected to continue in the near future (Dai, 2011; Goetz, Martínez, & Xabadia, 2017). Yet, the confidence associated with both the identification of a growing global trend in droughts and with its attribution to climate change can be low, as those findings are sensitive to the analytical instruments used to detect drought. Hence, there remains a query on how much these instruments are representative of the underlying physical processes (Sheffield, Wood, & Roderick, 2012).

Response actions to droughts tend to vary depending on the phase of the event, due to the slow build-up nature of the phenomenon. Simultaneously, they include diverse strategies in response to different sectoral impacts (Griggs, 2014). If developed well, water governance strategies, such as water allocation rules, can prove a satisfying adaptability to the occurrence of droughts while maintaining their effectiveness also in non-drought conditions (Goetz, Martínez, & Xabadia, 2017). Yet, the creeping nature of droughts makes it nearly impossible to actively manage and mitigate those weather extremes, posing a challenge to effective lesson drawing from previous events (Griggs, 2014). However, positive experiences of capacity building and increasing knowledge derivation from drought events occur, and they can aid in enhancing the preparedness of communities for future droughts (Griggs, 2014).

3.1.4.3 Water Variability

Water variability is a term that can be used to collectively refer to strong fluctuations in the water flow, which constitutes a problem from the social or environmental point of view. Variability can be detected in many components of the water cycle, and it can be considered in space, in time, or in both simultaneously (te Wierik et al., 2020). In some cases, the variability of the water cycle components provides important inputs for the functioning of ecosystems, as it can enhance nutrient cycles (Bischoff-Mattson & Lynch, 2016). However, most of the time, water variability is referred to as an issue, related to the unreliability it produces.

Some authors (e.g., Bischoff-Mattson & Lynch, 2016; Lopus et al., 2017) point out the interconnectedness of water variability and the water cycle itself. For instance, climate change increases the variability of meteorological forcings including rainfall (Lopus et al., 2017). Increased variability in water flow regime can translate into an increase of water extremes, such as floods and droughts. Highly variable flow regimes typically tend to interact with other types of drivers, exacerbating their effects, as can be seen in the case of semiarid zones, where climate change–driven variability in rainfall has been increasing the local vulnerability to dry spells and drought events (Bischoff-Mattson & Lynch, 2016; Mvungi, Mashauri, & Madulu, 2005). In this sense, water variability reduces the reliability of water resources as it decreases their stability in time and their homogeneity in space. The result of this lowered reliability of water resources can often be the increased competition for their use (Bischoff-Mattson & Lynch, 2016).

Moreover, variability in water availability and water cycle components can reduce the synergy between ecological and social resilience, putting strategies aimed at the preservation of water resources and strategies aimed at their fair distribution in contrast with each other (Romm, Conrad, & Måren, 2018). In terms of water governance, this often translates into a mismatch between the natural (highly variable) water regime and the desired characteristics of the water supply system functioning (Romm, Conrad, & Måren, 2018). This is often a trigger for prompting policies and governance structures aimed at regulating water supply and preventing water variability-associated risks, which ultimately increases the importance of water governance and water infrastructures in such contexts (Bischoff-Mattson & Lynch, 2016; Lopus et al., 2017). Beyond traditional governance and gray infrastructures, ecosystem restoration has been shown to have high potential in increasing resilience and fostering adaptation to climate and water variability (te Wierik et al., 2020).

3.1.5 Water Conflicts

There is an extensive and varied literature analyzing water conflicts. This derives, at least partially, from the wide scope of the definition of water conflicts itself. In principle, the governance of water as a finite resource must deal with different objectives, meaning that it intrinsically must deal with conflicting instances (Wolf, 2007). Indeed, water conflicts can range from conflicting interests over water use – for example, between different sectors, or between actors with different scopes, visions, or even ideologies on water use – to management issues on water resources that are shared among different territorial actors, but also to more violent outcomes of such tensions (Gober et al., 2014; Wolf, 2007).

Water conflicts have their roots in flawed water governance. The typical framing for water conflicts is that of tensions between rival water uses arising when water governance fails to address problems of water quality and quantity, food security, and water extremes (van der Zaag, Gupta, & Darvis, 2009). This can happen on multiple governance scales, as it can involve a variety of actors (state and non-state, individual and collective, etc.) (van der Zaag, Gupta, & Darvis, 2009). Yet, water conflicts are not equally frequent, or typical, across all scales of water governance. In fact, while a rich history of water conflicts has been reported globally, conflicts between state authorities over water as a scarce resource – that is, what are usually defined as 'water wars' and often occupy a prominent space in public opinion on water conflicts – have only a minute presence in historical records (Wolf, 2007).

While past water wars seem difficult to identify, there is uncertainty about whether climate and global changes may modify the way states approach problems of transboundary water governance, ultimately increasing the likelihood of water wars. Yet, even in regions of the world where this seems most possible, the water wars narrative still appears to be overstated (Zhang, 2016).

Water conflicts remain an important challenge of our times if we consider them as their initial definition – that is, as non-cooperative outcomes of flawed and tense water governance issues. Indeed, the framing of the dialectics of water governance processes, as well as their more or less explicit targets, are important in determining the outcomes of water governance issues (Gober et al., 2014). Understanding the shared objectives on tense interactions in water governance is crucial to be able to determine if these tensions will resolve in more cooperative or conflictual expressions (Bourdais Park, Adibayeva, & Saari, 2020).

One issue in this sense is that research has been focusing primarily on exploratively studying water conflicts, in a reiterated effort to find a quasi-universal framework, while focusing much less on finding and formalizing potential solution pathways to favor cooperative outcomes of flawed water governance, and to improve the governance capacity itself (van der Zaag, Gupta, & Darvis, 2009). This issue acquires an even greater importance in the light of the ineffectiveness and high costs of water conflicts as a form of resolution for tense water governance issues, making water conflicts prevention of crucial importance for sustainable development, especially in fragile contexts (Wolf, 2007).

3.1.6 Aquatic Deterioration

Degradation of aquatic ecosystems is a key human–water problématique that emerges from the SLR as composed by two main subclusters related to (1) ecosystem degradation and (2) eutrophication.

3.1.6.1 Ecosystem Degradation

The state of the world's ecosystems is a matter of grave concern, as highlighted in several scientific articles. Numerous authors describe how human activities, such as land use changes, infrastructures construction, and agricultural expansion and intensification, contribute to the deterioration of diverse types of aquatic ecosystems (Carpenter, Stanley, & vander Zanden, 2011; Castello & Macedo, 2016; Özerol, Bressers, & Coenen, 2012). Literature sheds light on the physical, chemical, and biological changes occurring in these vital ecosystems, demonstrating the severe consequences of degradation for biodiversity and the provision of essential ecosystem services (Carpenter, Stanley, & vander Zanden, 2011).

Providing an illustrative example, Castello and Macedo (2016) report the large-scale degradation observed in Amazonian freshwater ecosystems. The expansion of agriculture, deforestation, and infrastructure development have significantly impacted the region's rivers and their associated ecosystems. The loss of habitat and the alteration of natural flow patterns have led to the decline of unique species and disrupted ecosystem functioning. The Amazon, known for its remarkable biodiversity, is facing a critical challenge in maintaining the health and resilience of its freshwater ecosystems. The challenge of providing environmental flow rules to sustain river ecosystems further emphasizes the need for effective management (Arthington et al., 2006). The availability of adequate water flows is crucial for supporting aquatic life and maintaining the integrity of river ecosystems. However, finding a balance between water allocation for human needs, such as irrigation for agriculture, and the ecological requirements of rivers presents a complex task. The importance of managing environmental flows to ensure the long-term sustainability of these aquatic ecosystems cannot be overstated (Özerol, Bressers, & Coenen, 2012).

Investing in natural capital offers a promising avenue for improving ecosystem services (Ouyang et al. 2016). By recognizing the value of nature and the services it provides, we can enhance conservation efforts and promote sustainable practices. This approach involves aligning agricultural practices with environmental goals to minimize negative impacts on ecosystems. Investing in sustainable agricultural methods can reduce pollution, protect soil health, and preserve the integrity of aquatic ecosystems (Ouyang et al. 2016).

These interconnected themes highlight the urgency of addressing the problem of ecosystem degradation. It is essential to adopt holistic approaches that integrate scientific knowledge, policy interventions, and community engagement. By understanding the complex web of interactions between the physical, chemical, and biological components of ecosystems, it is possible to develop effective conservation and management strategies. Only through collaborative efforts, goals such as the mitigation of ecosystem degradation, restoration of ecological balance, and safeguarding of the invaluable services provided by ecosystems for present and future generations can be achieved.

3.1.6.2 Eutrophication

One of the leading stressors of global aquatic ecosystems, eutrophication refers to the degradation of water quality due to an oversaturation of water bodies with nutrients (Jetoo, 2018; Jetoo & Krantzberg, 2016). This nutrient enrichment can originate from both point and diffuse sources, including agriculture and fertilizer use, urban runoff, WWTPs, and industrial discharges (Dodds et al., 2009; Jetoo & Krantzberg, 2016; Schindler, 2006). Eutrophication manifests itself through widespread algal blooms due to an overload of predominantly nitrogen and phosphorus from agriculture and other human activities (Jetoo, 2018; Schindler, 2006).

Due to its complicated nature, eutrophication is deemed a wicked problem. As relevant information remains incomplete, solving this issue is a significant challenge. It is hard to deduct specific patterns due to conflicting findings, and the solutions are far from straightforward (Jetoo, 2018; Jetoo & Krantzberg, 2016). What is more, algal blooms have been on the rise in comparison with previous decades and, alongside eutrophication, these trends are expected to continue proliferating in the upcoming years (Heisler et al., 2008; Schindler, 2006).

As argued by some authors (e.g, Jetoo, 2018; Jetoo & Krantzberg, 2016), eutrophication is a consequence of poor governance. Therefore, some of the leading prescriptions to this problem are multilevel governance innovations and adaptive governance approaches, with elements such as public participation and flexibility, aimed at the goal of nutrient reduction. Simultaneously, there seems to be a consensus about the preference for proactive, rather than reactive, strategies to the problem (Heisler et al., 2008; Schindler, 2006).

3.1.7 Water (In)Security

Multiple definitions of the concept of water security can be found in academic, institutional, and policy literature since the paradigm has become widely used. A comprehensive review from Cook and Bakker (2012) shows how an initial focus on quantity and availability of water for multiple uses tended to move toward connotations including water quality, human health, and environmental issues. This shift serves as evidence that the paradigm developed within a wide range of sectors and across multiple disciplines, moving from natural to social and economic sciences (Cook & Bakker, 2012). Grey and Sadoff (2007) underline that water security, contrary to food and energy security, refers not only to the absence of the resource, but also to its presence, which can be a threat.

The UN refers to water security when the society is capable of having sustainable access to adequate and sufficient (both in terms of quantity and quality) water for sustaining livelihoods, human health, ecosystems, socioeconomic activities, and development while people, the environment, and economies coexist with an acceptable level of water-related risks. Researchers found that the global population exposed to high risk for water insecurity is around 80 percent (Vörösmarty et al., 2010).

Freshwater systems are increasingly threatened by human activities and human-induced climate changes over a wide range of spatial scales from local to global (Vörösmarty et al., 2010). An increasing population and economic development are, in fact, putting pressure not only on water quantity and availability but also on quality, with implications for other uses and the health of both humans and ecosystems (Wheater & Gober, 2015). Vörösmarty and coauthors (2010) argue that integrated water management strategies ought to consider balancing actions between human resource use and ecosystem protection to be successful. Since many stressors endanger the two actors through similar pathways, the protection of ecosystems and biodiversity is essential to ensuring human water security.

Carefully studying the paths followed by countries that have achieved water security suggests that this goal cannot be reached without social and environmental costs, being always necessary to deal with multiple and inevitable trade-offs, which may vary in different circumstances (Grey & Sadoff, 2007). When it comes to water security, water withdrawn for irrigation plays a relevant role, since the agricultural sector is responsible for up to 70 percent of freshwater use (de Loë & Bjornlund, 2008). Irrigation, in fact, contributes to global food security, which is strictly related to water security. At the same time, irrigation requires constant improvement and renovations to avoid water management problems, while water allocation is essential for enhancing water security. A successful strategy should be based on economic instruments accompanied by improved governance.

3.1.8 Water–Energy–Food Nexus

Energy, water, and food policy have numerous interwoven concerns, and understanding their interrelationships is crucial for targeting synergies and avoiding tensions. Economic and security-related concerns are emerging as strong drivers for change alongside environmental issues (Bazilian et al., 2011). The water–energy–food (WEF) nexus refers to the interconnectedness among water, energy, and food resources (Endo et al., 2017). It recognizes the inextricable linkages between these resources and the need for integrated approaches to their management. Through system thinking, the WEF nexus develops integrated indices, models, and methods for analyzing and understanding trade-offs among water, energy, and food (Bazilian et al., 2011; Endo et al., 2017).

Many projects and initiatives have been implemented worldwide, driven by different interests, often focusing on water-related activities such as agriculture, wastewater treatment, and hydropower generation. The nexus concept also encompasses social and governance activities combined with environmental and economic research (Endo et al., 2017). Yet, while the nexus is recognized at the research level, its implementation on the ground remains limited, requiring more involvement from non-research communities (Endo et al., 2017). Indeed, a functioning WEF nexus approach requires breaking down silos and rethinking policy and management approaches (Greer, Hannibal, & Portney, 2020). However, the lack of communication and coordination between water, energy, and food policy areas is still evident (Greer, Hannibal, & Portney, 2020).

Politically, the security language used in WEF nexus discourses to address environmental problems and policies may move economic productivity to the focus of policies, shifting authority from state-centric institutions to private-sector organizations (Liebenguth, 2020). Nonetheless, the transformative potential of the WEF nexus lies in addressing resource management challenges through self-organization and design of governance systems (Pahl-Wostl, 2019). In this sense, the WEF nexus holds potential for achieving the Sustainable Development Goals and ensuring the resilience and security of water, energy, and food resources (Pahl-Wostl, 2019; Endo et al., 2017).

3.1.9 Water, Sanitation, and Hygiene

Improving access to water, sanitation, and hygiene (WASH) globally has been listed as "one of the least expensive and most effective means to improve public health and save lives" (Montgomery & Elimelech, 2007, p. 17). However, inadequate WASH is still listed as one of the leading global threats, despite improvements over the years (Prüss-Ustün et al., 2019).

A key element when striving for improved WASH is adequate governance, including strategic and sustainable policymaking and planning with the involvement of local communities and other relevant stakeholders (Cumming & Cairncross, 2016; Montgomery & Elimelech, 2007; Motta-Veiga, 2021). The benefits of effective WASH interventions go beyond health, including increased privacy and convenience, which has been linked to the risk of violence (Cumming & Cairncross, 2016).

Access to safe WASH is often linked to child development (e.g., Cumming & Cairncross, 2016; Ngure et al., 2014; Prüss-Ustün et al., 2019). As shown by Ngure et al. (2014), the disease burden related to poor WASH services falls disproportionately on children in low-income countries. Similarly, access to water and sanitation services remains a problem predominantly for the poor communities in low-income countries, with sub-Saharan Africa and South Asia listed as areas with the largest deficits (Cumming & Cairncross, 2016; Motta-Veiga, 2021). Some authors (e.g., Cumming & Cairncross, 2016) scale down their focus, underscoring the disparities in access to WASH services between urban and rural areas.

4 Discussion

4.1 Co-occurrences of Problématiques in Scientific Literature

Water issues are intrinsically complex and have been recognized as a type of wicked problem, which are characterized by diverging perspectives, values, understandings, and interests (Zwarteveen et al., 2017). Thus, the contemporary waterspace is difficult to navigate, as water challenges are characterized by a visible interconnectivity and reciprocity, where one problem can be linked to or even serve as an underlying cause for another issue (Brennan et al., 2021; Cooley et al., 2013; Jury & Vaux, 2007; Li, Endter-Wada & Li, 2015; Ozbekhan, 1970; Woodhouse & Muller, 2017).

This complexity and interconnectedness are reflected in the findings of this study. As shown in Figure 6, the analyzed water governance literature is characterized by a range of co-occurrences of problématiques and their sub-clusters. This figure has been developed based on the problématiques database developed as a result of this research, where each of the shortlisted sources has

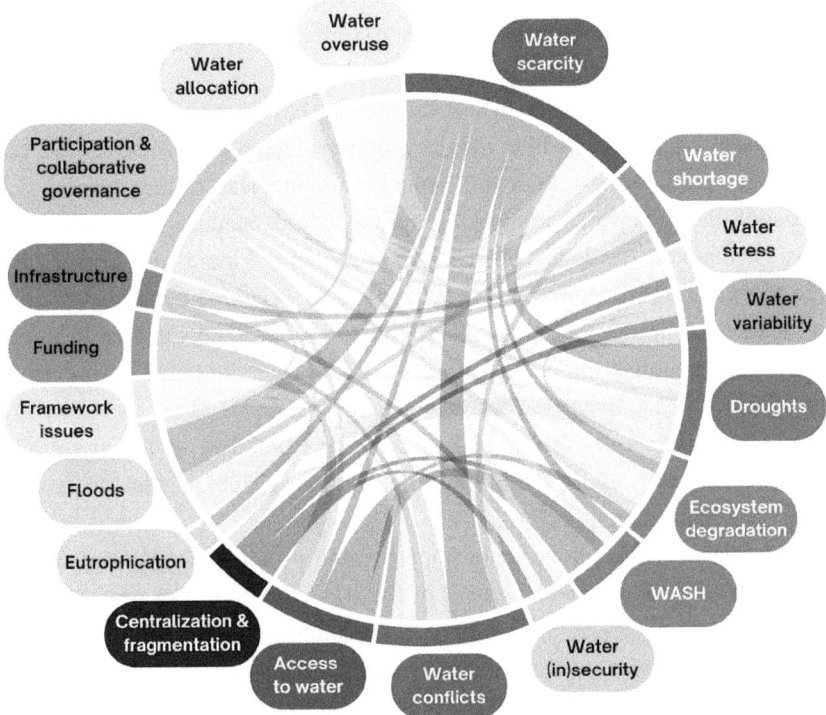

Figure 6 Diagram representing the co-occurrences of problématiques in scientific literature.

been coded according to the specific problem(s) it discusses. Due to the complexity of the water issues, in most cases, the analyzed publications would focus on more than one problem (see Appendix A).

These interlinkages have been documented in the wider water governance literature. There is a great body of literature discussing the internal connections within the water quantity problématique. Authors such as Alcamo, Flörke, and Märker (2007) and Wada and Bierkens (2014) discuss the links between water scarcity, stress, shortage, and (over)use. Moving beyond this problématique, Rijsberman (2006) and Richey et al. (2015) link water conflicts to water quantity issues. Another prevalent connection is the one between infrastructure and water investments (Briscoe, 1999; Rodriguez, van den Berg, & McMahon, 2012; Zhao, Fonseca, & Zeerak, 2019). This overlap had been further linked to the issue of water affordability and water access (Obeng-Odoom, 2012).

4.2 What Solutions? Is it Possible to Move Beyond Panaceas?

As mentioned at the start of this Element, water governance scholarship provides an abundance of scientific knowledge relevant in the face of the ongoing water crisis. However, arguably due to the lack of synthesis of the available information, solutions are lagging behind (Graffy, 2006; Grigg, 2021; Jury & Vaux, 2005; Pahl-Wostl, 2017).

It is crucial to echo what many critical scholars have been emphasizing in the recent years – that is, the call to move beyond the idea of panaceas, believed to be the metaphoric 'one-size-fits-all' remedies. At the heart of this research lies the belief that each water problem, alongside its understanding and ideal solutions, is context dependent. This research takes Jamie Linton's (2010) memorable statement of "water is what we make of it" (p. ix) in our belief that there is no objective definition of the global water crisis – our understanding is highly dynamic, depending on our relationship with water and, borrowing from Querejazu (2022), "what the water is doing" (p. 181). Thus, as shown by decades of failures of institutional prescriptions believed to be universally applicable, as well as in words of Elinor Ostrom (2008), "quick fixes may cause more harm than good" (p. 14).

At the basis of the taxonomy of human–water problématiques presented in this Element is the acknowledgment of the wicked nature of water problems (Markowska et al., 2020; Sanya, 2020). The complexity and the interconnectedness of water issues pose a major challenge when searching for effective solutions. One approach that has received significant attention in the last decades is decentralization, where the responsibility for tackling a complex issue is redistributed across an array of actors (Pahl-Wostl & Knieper, 2014).

The proclaimed effectiveness of this approach stems from the opportunity to divide the task at hand into simpler and solvable problem components to be assigned across the diverse actors involved (Edelenbos & Teisman, 2011).

This guidance is strongly linked to the idea of inclusive participation and collaboration in water governance processes. Here, some authors emphasize the need to build bridges across sectors (e.g., moving beyond research and academia, as argued by Endo et al., 2017) and scalar levels (as shown in the case of the EU's WFD or the Clean Water Act in the USA). In a similar vein, a participatory approach is one of the key elements underlying the basic idea of IWRM – a comprehensive consideration of water that suggests the management of the resource across all sectors, with a wide variety of actors participating in the decision-making processes (Giordano & Shah, 2014). The emphasis on participatory approaches became one of the central pillars of the 1992 Dublin principles, as well as one of the qualities of 'effective water governance,' as defined by the Global Water Partnership in their 2003 report (Lautze et al., 2011; Rogers & Hall, 2003; Roque et al., 2022; Solanes & Gonzalez-Villareal, 1999). It is also at the basis of highly contested, yet continuously influential, IWRM approach to water management (Giordano & Shah, 2014; Lautze et al., 2011).

Some authors (e.g., Cumming & Cairncross, 2016; Moe & Rheingans, 2006; Vásquez & Franceschi, 2013) underline the necessity of public participation – that is, involvement of citizens and/or local communities in decision-making and in 'doing' water governance. Such inclusive approaches would ensure an increasingly comprehensive understanding of problems on hand, resulting in improved conceptualization of a given issue and, in consequence, in better solutions (Blackstock & Richards, 2007; Roque et al., 2022).

Another interesting consequence of public participation is the increased rate of innovation, as argued by Wehn et al. (2015). Some authors (e.g., di Baldassarre et al., 2013) note the reliance on nuanced and unconventional water governance practices as potential solutions to the encountered human–water problems. This transition to innovative approaches appears to be a necessity, as the mainstream water governance practices were proved to be ill-equipped to effectively cope with the growing pressures on water resources (Dellapenna et al., 2013). At the same time, it has been noted that wicked problems are unsolvable through the use of conventional, linear approaches (Lach, Rayner, & Ingram, 2005; Markowska et al., 2020; Rittel & Webber, 1973; Sanya, 2020). Therefore, innovation can be seen as a necessity when working toward effective solutions to wicked problems of the current waterscape. At the same time, it is crucial to apply a flexible approach and remain adaptive, in particular when tackling issues whose short- and long-term consequences are unknown (Heisler et al., 2008; Moss, 2012). Yet, despite potential uncertainties, there ought to be a shared understanding of rules amongst all involved to remain effective when engaging in multi-actor processes (Pahl-Wostl & Knieper, 2014).

Nevertheless, as stressed by authors such as Imperial (2005), collaborative and participatory governance ought not to be seen as a panacea. Moreover, several authors (e.g., Argade & Narayanan, 2019; Cuadrado-Quesada & Schwartz, 2022; Roth et al., 2017) underscore the challenges associated with participation and collaborative approaches to water governance. These difficulties for a successful creation of collaborative governance regimes include the differences in how a given water problem is comprehended, the tensions between nurturing local autonomy and establishing a regional approach, the aversion toward cooperation amongst certain actors, and the influence of personal preferences and interests reflected in shaping agendas, as well as the issue of depoliticization of water problems at stake (Cain, Gerber, & Hui, 2020; Kastens & Newig, 2008; Rana & Piracha, 2018; Roth et al., 2017; Souvik Ghosh et al., 2008). Other scholars (e.g., Giordano & Shah, 2014) maintain that participation is not always necessary. In a similar vein, some argue that participation is at risk of becoming "implacably emptied of meaning" (Cornwall & Brock, 2005, p. 1056), turning into no more than a buzzword (Leal, 2007).

Another point shared by many authors is the need for a paradigm shift. For some (e.g., Gohari et al., 2013; Kummu et al., 2010; Mancosu et al., 2015; Pimentel et al., 2004), this is exemplified by a shift to nonstructural 'soft' approaches that focus on increased resilience and efficiency. For others (e.g., Ahlers et al., 2014), the transition ought to include how we understand water itself, moving beyond material functionality of water, emphasizing the cultural, symbolic, and spiritual dimensions. In line with this view, this move should lead to the acceptance of nontraditional worldviews that might be incompatible with conventional practices currently imposed as 'good governance.'

4.3 Blind Spots and Possible Additional Problématiques: Old Wine in a Bigger Bottle?

Underlying this research is the ontological question of what defines a problem. When scanning the literature obtained through the process of an SLR, it has become apparent that while the majority of water governance literature concerns itself with concepts that could be conventionally classified as problems (i.e., straightforward empirical issues such as water scarcity or wetland destruction), a portion of the scholarship focuses on themes that do not fit this mainstream definition of a problem. This latter body of literature discusses themes such as water justice, framing of water problems and solutions, plurality of views in water governance (or lack thereof), the inclusion and/or exclusion of marginalized voices, and challenging the dominant paradigms – a more elusive and less material category of problems (e.g., Bond, 2013; Gerlak, Louder, & Ingram, 2022; Lynch et al., 2013; Neto, 2016; Wilk et al., 2017; Yates et al., 2005; Zegwaard & Wester, 2014).

This reflection falls in line with research conducted by Brennan et al. (2021), who propose a problem language context (PLC) model to frame and, in consequence, understand sustainable development challenges, including water problems. Through the application of the PLC model, the authors examine how water problems are represented at different levels of analysis. The idea to organize findings according to the conceptual techniques of levels has a rather rich history going back several decades, a summary of which is distinctively offered by Brennan et al. (2021). When analyzing problem representation, the first step is to distinguish between different categories of questioning: (1) 'What exists?'; (2) 'What are we capable of doing?'; (3) 'What is it that we want to do?'; and (4) 'What we must do OR how to do what we want to do?', as listed by the authors. Each of these questions suggests a unique manner of perceiving and classifying problems, ranging from empirical issues such as water pollution (in response to the first category of questioning) to values-based problems including the human right to water (fourth category) (Brennan et al., 2021).

Relying on this process of problem representation allows us to distinguish between different types of problems. Such a distinction can serve as the conceptual foundation for expanding the problématiques taxonomy, as it considers issues that fall beyond the empirical understanding of a problem. Therefore, this could allow for notions such as water justice and inclusion of marginalized voices to be considered alongside the challenges listed in the Section 3.1, which remains a relevant step for further research. This reflection is in line with the previously mentioned acknowledgment of the limitations of this research – with solely English-language sources used as the basis of this study, it was never aimed at a definitive explanation of the building blocks of the global water crisis. We recognize the strong Western bias and highlight the valuable contributions of critical water governance scholarship of the recent years. Moreover, the attempt to "capture water in a fix translatable word" (Querejazu, 2022, p. 181) and, by extension, claiming to offer exhaustive definition of the global water crisis is futile, as water, as well as our understanding of it, and the related problems are ever-changing and ever-flowing.

The focus on the aforementioned problems that go beyond the material definition of water challenges can be seen as a proof of the evolution of the water governance field, reflected by the thematic expansion of the scholarship. Indeed, the inclusion of such themes can be seen as a relatively recent phenomenon. As can be seen in the problématiques database, sources listed in these clusters have been published almost exclusively in the last ten years.

This finding offers an interesting response to the "Too much and not enough" *Nature Sustainability* editorial, which argues that "in recent years, some scholars have started to wonder if water studies research has become a bit, well, stagnant" (*Nature Sustainability* Editorial Board, 2021, p. 659). Our findings appear to be in line with the response written by Venot et al. (2022), who assert that the editorial does not consider emerging fields of water studies such as socio-hydrology (e.g., Sivapalan, Savenije, & Bloschl, 2012), hydro-sociology (e.g., Rangecroft et al., 2021), hydro-politics (e.g., Grandi, 2020), and water governance studies (e.g., Woodhouse & Muller, 2017). These emerging disciplines are dynamically pushing the boundaries of interdisciplinary water research by integrating a focus on water issues with critical epistemologies, introducing quantitative approaches to complement sociopolitical analyses of water, and engaging with both realities and representations of water, drawing on established research traditions such as political ecology, critical geography, and postcolonial studies (Macura-Nnamdi & Sikora, 2023; Venot et al., 2022). Through this, the new currents in studying water reflect its resistance to the "disciplinarian compartmentalization of distinct sciences and practices of knowledge" (Macura-Nnamdi & Sikora, 2023, p. 6).

Indeed, a growing number of critical scholars bring the importance of the sociopolitical side of water problems to our attention. Aptly argued by Mehta and Nicol (2023), the reliance on "apocalyptic framings" (para. 10) shifts the focus away from the more challenging issues linked to power dynamics, marginalization, and more. Similarly, Molle, Lankford, and Lave (2024) point out that the use of quantitative outputs tends to conceal "deeply political processes, hypotheses, worldviews, intents, old habits and new fashions" (p. 326). This increasing recognition of plurality of nature of human–water problems continues to challenge the more mainstream perspectives.

This emergence of critical water governance studies and the introduction of new perspectives can explain the proliferation of scientific papers where water problems are understood in a broader and less tangible manner. At the same time, the more critical perspectives challenge the established dominant paradigms, while posing crucial questions, such as '*who* is doing the defining?' A growing number of scholars recognize the political nature of governing water, as well as the underlying power dynamics of processes such as concept defining (e.g., Zwarteveen et al., 2017). In consequence, this heightened inclusion of critical perspectives invites a deeper reflection of what constitutes water problems, which remains a relevant avenue for future research. At the same time, it is worth acknowledging that these 'additional' problems are in fact not new, yet their recognition is. Problems of justice, alternative worldviews, and others did exist before; however, they did not fit into the dominant paradigm in Western scholarship. This brings to mind the parable of 'old wine in a new bottle' – or rather, following this reflection, old wine in a bigger, more inclusive metaphoric bottle.

5 Conclusion

The concept of the global water crisis has been steadily proliferating across water governance literature in recent decades (e.g., Biswas & Tortajada, 2023; Dellapenna et al., 2013; Jury & Vaux, 2007; Moe & Rheingans, 2006). Despite its growing presence, defining this notion remains a challenge, as it has become an umbrella term applied to an array of problems (Srinivasan et al., 2012). This is due to the ambiguous definition of water crisis, where diverse authors rely on their own understanding of the term. This underscores the challenge of interpreting the existing data, while keeping a comprehensive perspective. In this sense, the perceptions of the global water crisis bring to mind the Buddhist parable of the blind men and an elephant, where each definition is based on specific, yet limited viewpoints (Ireland, 2007).

This task of defining and interpreting remains a challenge, as the contemporary waterscape appears to lack a synthesis of the most pressing water problems (van der Zaag, Gupta, & Darvis, 2009). Moreover, contemporary water issues are of interconnected and wicked nature, signifying that one problem can be linked to or even serve as an underlying cause for another issue. Clarity about the nature of the ongoing water crisis would allow for an effective communication of water challenges with policymakers and practitioners, as well as the wider society, helping set priorities for future-oriented and resilient water governance.

This research undertook the task of synthesizing the water governance scholarship to identify the key human–water problems to help navigate this complex waterscape. Nine key human–water problématiques were obtained as a result of an SLR review and a CCM: (1) water governance problématique; (2) water quantity problématique; (3) water quality problématique; (4) weather extremes problématqiues; (5) water conflicts problématiques; (6) ecosystem degradation problématique; (7) water (in)security problématique; (8) water–energy–food problématique; and (9) water, sanitation, and hygiene problématique. Together, these constitute the taxonomy of human–water problématiques.

This research offers a novel contribution in the face of the progressing water crisis. Coherently synthesizing and displaying key pressures within the water realm, it points a way forward for prioritizing and agenda-setting.

Simultaneously, the database created for the purpose of this paper offers insights into the evolution of our understanding of what a water problem is. Whilst the early portion of water governance scholarship concerns itself with empirical problems, such as water scarcity, the more recent publications take on themes that do not fit into such conventional definition of water issues. This latter body of literature discusses themes such as water justice, framing of water problems and solutions, and plurality of views in water governance (or lack thereof), suggesting a transformation of the water governance field (e.g., Bond, 2013; Gerlak, Louder, & Ingram, 2022; Lynch et al., 2013; Neto, 2016; Wilk et al., 2017; Yates et al., 2005; Zegwaard & Wester, 2014).

With the efforts to present global human–water problems in an integrated manner, this research provided a broader overview of the complexity of defining the global water crisis, which hopefully can be useful for scholars as well as for practitioners and policymakers. The taxonomy of human–water problématiques serves as the first step toward cumulative and targeted global action for water, with the ambitious goal of contributing to the improvement of our water governance practices and addressing the challenges of the 'global water crisis.' However, it is crucial to return to the acknowledgment that one's understanding of water is highly contextual and dynamic. This research recognizes that uncovering the nature of water crisis is an ongoing process, and thus attempting to give a definitive and exhaustive overview is a futile task, as argued by Macura-Nnamdi and Sikora (2023), who, referring to Wisława Szymborska's *Water*, point to "the impossibility to grasp the abundant materiality of water and to the inadequacy of language to keep up with its fugitive realities and shapes" (p. 3). Water overruns rigid definitions and attempts to enclose it with paradigmatic thinking.

As the global water crisis has become a current international agenda priority, such attempts to enclose water and water problems in clearly delineated bounds are not uncommon. Depending on the definition of what the global water crisis is, resources will be mobilized, narratives defined, and certain interests prioritized over others. Therefore, considering that environmental (and water) narratives can be mobilized to achieve specific political or speculative goals, providing analytical meaning to this broad, equally ambiguous, yet urgent issue is a necessity. On the one hand, this review showed that defining the global water crisis entails engaging with conceptual complexities. On the other hand, it stressed that reductionist answers fall short and are there for a reason, with clearly understandable, if scrutinized, societal, political, and economic implications.

References

Ahlers, R., Cleaver, F., Rusca, M., & Schwartz, K. (2014). Informal space in the urban waterscape: Disaggregation and co-production of water services. *Water Alternatives*, *7*(1), pp. 1–14. www.water-alternatives.org/index.php/volume7/v7issue1/230-a7-1-1/file.

Alcamo, J., Flörke, M., & Märker, M. (2007). Future long-term changes in global water resources driven by socio-economic and climatic changes. *Hydrological Sciences Journal*, *52*(2), pp. 247–275. http://doi.org/10.1623/hysj.52.2.247.

Amarante, V., Burger, R., Chelwa, G., et al. (2022). Underrepresentation of developing country researchers in development research. *Applied Economics Letters*, *29*(17), pp. 1659–1664. https://doi.org/10.1080/13504851.2021.1965528.

Amineh, R. J., & Asl, H. D. (2015). Review of constructivism and social constructivism. *Journal of Social Sciences, Literature and Languages*, *1*(1), pp. 9–16.

Argade, P., & Narayanan, N. C. (2019). Undercurrents of participatory groundwater governance in Rural Jalna, Western India. *Western India: Water Alternatives*, *12*(3), pp. 869–885.

Arnell, N. W. (2004). Climate change and global water resources: SRES emissions and socio-economic scenarios. *Global Environmental Change*, *14*(1), pp. 31–52. http://doi.org/10.1016/j.gloenvcha.2003.10.006.

Arthington, A. H., Bunn, S. E., Poff, N. L., & Naiman, R. J. (2006). The challenge of providing environmental flow rules to sustain river ecosystems. *Ecological Applications*, *16*(4), pp. 1311–1318. https://doi.org/10.1890/1051-0761(2006)016[1311:TCOPEF]2.0.CO;2.

Aydin, A., Yürük, S. E., Reisoğlu, İ., & Goktas, Y. (2023). Main barriers and possible enablers of academicians while publishing. *Scientometrics*, *128*(1), pp. 623–650. https://doi.org/10.1007/s11192-022-04528-x.

Bai, Y. (2018). Has the Global South become a playground for Western scholars in information and communication technologies for development? Evidence from a three-journal analysis. *Scientometrics*, *116*(3), pp. 2139–2153. https://doi.org/10.1007/s11192-018-2839-y.

Baird, J., Plummer, R., Dupont, D., & Carter, B. (2015). Berghahn Books perceptions of water quality in First Nations communities: Exploring the role of context. *Nature and Culture*, *10*(2), pp. 225–249. http://doi.org/10.2307/26206074.

Bazilian, M., Rogner, H., Howells, M., et al. (2011). Considering the energy, water and food nexus: Towards an integrated modelling approach. *Energy Policy*, *39*(12), pp. 7896–7906. http://doi.org/10.1016/j.enpol.2011.09.039.

Bilalova, S., Newig, J., & Villamayor-Tomas, S. (2025). Toward sustainable water governance? Taking stock of paradigms, practices, and sustainability outcomes. *Wiley Interdisciplinary Reviews: Water*, *12*(1), e1762. https://doi.org/10.1002/wat2.1762.

Bischoff-Mattson, Z., & Lynch, A. H. (2016). Adaptive governance in water reform discourses of the Murray–Darling Basin, Australia. *Policy Sciences*, *49*(3), pp. 281–307. http://doi.org/10.1007/s11077-016-9245-1.

Biswas, A. K. (2004). Integrated water resources management: A reassessment: A water forum contribution. *Water International*, *29*(2), pp. 248–256. http://doi.org/10.1080/02508060408691775.

Biswas, A. K., & Tortajada, C. (2019). Water crisis and water wars: Myths and realities. *International Journal of Water Resources Development*, *35*(5), pp. 727–731. http://doi.org/10.1080/07900627.2019.1636502.

Biswas, A. K., & Tortajada, C. (2023). Global crisis in water management: Can a second UN Water Conference help? *River*, *2*(2), pp. 143–148. http://doi.org/10.1002/rvr2.40.

Blackstock, K. L., & Richards, C. (2007). Evaluating stakeholder involvement in river basin planning: A Scottish case study. *Water Policy*, *9*(5), pp. 493–512. http://doi.org/10.2166/wp.2007.018.

Bond, P. (2013). Water rights, commons, and advocacy narratives. *South African Journal on Human Rights*, *29*(1), pp. 125–143. http://doi.org/10.1080/19962126.2013.11865068.

Bourdais Park, J. W., Adibayeva, A., & Saari, D. (2020). Contestation and collaboration for water resources: Comparing the emerging regional water governance of the Aral Sea, Irtysh River, and Mekong River. *Journal of Asian and African Studies*, *56*(6), pp. 1121–1143. http://doi.org/10.1177/0021909620957689.

Bremer, L. L., Auerbach, D. A., Goldstein, J. H., et al. (2016). One size does not fit all: Natural infrastructure investments within the Latin American Water Funds Partnership. *Ecosystem Services*, *17*, pp. 217–236. http://doi.org/10.1016/j.ecoser.2015.12.006.

Brennan, M., Rondón-Sulbarán, J., Sabogal-Paz, L. P., Fernandez-Ibañez, P., & Galdos-Balzategui, A. (2021). Conceptualising global water challenges: A transdisciplinary approach for understanding different discourses in sustainable development. *Journal of Environmental Management*, *298*, 113361. http://doi.org/10.1016/j.jenvman.2021.113361.

Briscoe, J. (1999). The changing face of water infrastructure financing in developing countries. *International Journal of Water Resources Development*, *15*(3), pp. 301–308. http://doi.org/10.1080/07900629948826.

Butler, C., & Pidgeon, N. (2011). From 'flood defence' to 'flood risk management': Exploring governance, responsibility, and blame. *Environment and Planning C: Government and Policy*, *29*(3), pp. 533–547. http://doi.org/10.1068/c09181j.

Cain, B. E., Gerber, E. R., & Hui, I. (2020). The challenge of externally generated collaborative governance: California's attempt at regional water management. *American Review of Public Administration*, *50*(4–5), pp. 428–437. http://doi.org/10.1177/0275074020908578.

Calzada, J., Iranzo, S., & Sanz, A. (2017). Community-managed water services. *The Journal of Environment & Development*, *26*(4), pp. 400–428. http://doi.org/10.2307/26392660.

Carey, R. O., & Migliaccio, K. W. (2009). Contribution of wastewater treatment plant effluents to nutrient dynamics in aquatic systems: A review. *Environmental Management*, *44*, pp. 205–217.

Carpenter, S. R., Stanley, E. H., & vander Zanden, M. J. (2011). State of the world's freshwater ecosystems: Physical, chemical, and biological changes. *Annual Review of Environment and Resources*, *36*, pp. 75–99. http://doi.org/10.1146/annurev-environ-021810-094524.

Carr, S. A., Liu, J., & Tesoro, A. G. (2016). Transport and fate of microplastic particles in wastewater treatment plants. *Water Research*, *91*, pp. 174–182.

Castello L., & Macedo M. N. (2016). Large-scale degradation of Amazonian freshwater ecosystems. *Global Change Biology*, *22*(3), pp. 990–1007. http://doi.org/10.1111/gcb.13173.

Collyer, F. M. (2018). Global patterns in the publishing of academic knowledge: Global North, global South. *Current Sociology*, *66*(1), pp. 56–73. https://doi.org/10.1177/0011392116680020.

Cook, C., & Bakker, K. (2012). Water security: Debating an emerging paradigm. *Global Environmental Change*, *22*(1), pp. 94–102. http://doi.org/10.1016/j.gloenvcha.2011.10.011.

Cooley, H., Ajami, N., Ha, M.-L., et al. (2013). *Global Water Governance in the 21st Century*. Oakland, CA: Pacific Institute for Studies in Development, Environment, and Security.

Cornwall, A., & Brock, K. (2005). What do buzzwords do for development policy? A critical look at 'participation,' 'empowerment' and 'poverty reduction.' *Third World Quarterly*, *26*(7), pp. 1043–1060. http://doi.org/10.1080/01436590500235603.

Cuadrado-Quesada, G., & Schwartz, K. (2022). Governing groundwater excess: Insights from a failed collaborative process in Delft, the Netherlands. *International Journal of Water Resources Development*, *38*(3), pp. 388–402. http://doi.org/10.1080/07900627.2021.1902285.

Cumming, O., & Cairncross, S. (2016). Can water, sanitation and hygiene help eliminate stunting? Current evidence and policy implications. *Maternal and Child Nutrition*, *12*(1), pp. 91–105. http://doi.org/10.1111/mcn.12258.

Dai, A. (2011). Drought under global warming: A review. *Wiley Interdisciplinary Reviews: Climate Change*, *2*(1), pp. 45–65. http://doi.org/10.1002/wcc.81.

del Moral, L., & Do Ó, A. (2014). Water governance and scalar politics across multiple-boundary river basins: States, catchments, and regional powers in the Iberian Peninsula. *Water International*, *39*(3), pp. 333–347. http://doi.org/10.1080/02508060.2013.878816.

de Loë, R. C., & Bjornlund, H. (2008). Irrigation and water security: The role of economic instruments and governance. *WIT Transactions on Ecology and the Environment*, *112*, pp. 35–42. http://doi.org/10.2495/SI080041.

Dell'Angelo, J., Rulli, M. C., & D'Odorico, P. (2018). The global water grabbing syndrome. *Ecological Economics*, *143*, pp. 276–285. https://doi.org/10.1016/j.ecolecon.2017.06.033.

Dellapenna, J. W., Gupta, J., Li, W., & Schmidt, F. (2013). Thinking about the future of global water governance. *Ecology and Society*, *18*(3), p. 28. http://doi.org/10.5751/ES-05657-180328.

Dewulf, A., Mancero, M., Cárdenas, G., & Sucozhañay, D. (2011). Fragmentation and connection of frames in collaborative water governance: A case study of river catchment management in Southern Ecuador. *International Review of Administrative Sciences*, *77*(1), pp. 50–75. http://doi.org/10.1177/0020852310390108.

di Baldassarre, G., Kooy, M., Kemerink, J. S., & Brandimarte, L. (2013). Towards understanding the dynamic behaviour of floodplains as human–water systems. *Hydrology and Earth System Sciences*, *17*(8), pp. 3235–3244. http://doi.org/10.5194/hess-17-3235-2013.

Dodds, W. K., Bouska, W. W., Eitzmann, J. L., et al. (2009). Eutrophication of US freshwaters: Analysis of potential economic damages. *Environmental Science and Technology*, *43*(1), pp. 12–19. http://doi.org/10.1021/es801217q.

D'Odorico, P., Carr, J., Dalin, C., et al. (2019). Global virtual water trade and the hydrological cycle: Patterns, drivers, and socio-environmental impacts. *Environmental Research Letters*, *14*(5), 053001. http://doi.org/10.1088/1748-9326/ab05f4.

D'Odorico, P., Dell'Angelo, J., & Rulli, M. C. (2024). Water commons grabbing and (in) justice. *Nature Water*, *2*(4), pp. 300–302. https://doi.org/10.1038/s44221-024-00231-8.

Edelenbos, J., & Teisman, G. R. (2011). Symposium on water governance. Prologue: Water governance as a government's actions between the reality of fragmentation and the need for integration. *International Review of Administrative Sciences*, *77*(1), pp. 5–30. http://doi.org/10.1177/0020852310390090.

Endo, A., Tsurita, I., Burnett, K., & Orencio, P. M. (2017). A review of the current state of research on the water, energy, and food nexus. *Journal of Hydrology: Regional Studies*, *11*, pp. 20–30. http://doi.org/10.1016/j.ejrh.2015.11.010.

Eneng, R., Lulofs, K., & Asdak, C. (2018). Towards a water balanced utilization through circular economy. *Management Research Review*, *41*(5), pp. 572–585. http://doi.org/10.1108/MRR-02-2018-0080.

Fallon, A. L., Lankford, B. A., & Weston, D. (2021). Navigating wicked water governance in the 'solutionscape' of science, policy, practice, and participation. *Ecology and Society*, *26*(2), p. 37. http://doi.org/10.5751/ES-12504-260237.

Franco, J., Mehta, L., & Veldwisch, G. J. (2013). The global politics of water grabbing. *Third World Quarterly*, *34*(9), pp. 1651–1675.

Funtowicz, S. O., & Ravetz, J. R. (1993). Science for the post-normal age. *Futures*, *25*(7), pp. 739–755. https://doi.org/10.1016/0016-3287(93)90022-L.

Funtowicz, S. O., & Ravetz, J. R. (1994). Uncertainty, complexity and post-normal science. *Environmental Toxicology and Chemistry*, *13*(12), pp. 1881–1885. http://doi.org/10.1002/etc.5620131203.

Garrick, D., Siebentritt, M. A., Aylward, B., Bauer, C. J., & Purkey, A. (2009). Water markets and freshwater ecosystem services: Policy reform and implementation in the Columbia and Murray–Darling basins. *Ecological Economics*, *69*(2), pp. 366–379. http://doi.org/10.1016/j.ecolecon.2009.08.004.

GCEW (2023). *About*. https://watercommission.org/about/.

Gerlak, A. K., Louder, E., & Ingram, H. (2022). Viewpoint: An intersectional approach to water equity in the US. *Water Alternatives*, *15*(1), pp. 1–12.

Giordano, M., & Shah, T. (2014). From IWRM back to integrated water resources management. *International Journal of Water Resources Development*, *30*(3), pp. 364–376. http://doi.org/10.1080/07900627.2013.851521.

Gober, P. A., Strickert, G. E., Clark, D. A., et al. (2014). Divergent perspectives on water security: Bridging the policy debate. *Professional Geographer*, *67*(1), pp. 62–71. http://doi.org/10.1080/00330124.2014.883960.

Goetz, R. U., Martínez, Y., & Xabadia, À. (2017). Efficiency and acceptance of new water allocation rules: The case of an agricultural water users association. *Science of the Total Environment*, *601–602*, pp. 614–625. http://doi.org/10.1016/j.scitotenv.2017.05.226.

Gohari, A., Eslamian, S., Mirchi, A., et al. (2013). Water transfer as a solution to water shortage: A fix that can Backfire. *Journal of Hydrology*, *491*(1), pp. 23–39. http://doi.org/10.1016/j.jhydrol.2013.03.021.

Goldman-Benner, R. L., Benitez, S., Boucher, T., et al. (2012). Water funds and payments for ecosystem services: Practice learns from theory and theory can learn from practice. *ORYX*, *46*(1), pp. 55–63. http://doi.org/10.1017/S0030605311001050.

Gomez, C. J., Herman, A. C., & Parigi, P. (2022). Leading countries in global science increasingly receive more citations than other countries doing similar research. *Nature Human Behaviour*, *6*(7), pp. 919–929. https://doi.org/10.1038/s41562-022-01351-5.

Graffy, E. A. (2006). Expert forecasts and the emergence of water scarcity on public agendas. *Society and Natural Resources*, *19*(5), pp. 465–472. http://doi.org/10.1080/08941920600561173.

Grafton, R. Q. (2017). Responding to the 'wicked problem' of water insecurity. *Water Resources Management*, *31*(10), pp. 3023–3041. http://doi.org/10.1007/s11269-017-1606-9.

Grandi, M. (2020). Hydropolitics. *Oxford Research Encyclopedia of Environmental Science*. Oxford: Oxford University Press. http://doi.org/10.1093/acrefore/9780199389414.013.644.

Greer, R. A., Hannibal, B., & Portney, K. (2020). The role of communication in managing complex water-energy-food governance systems. *Water (Switzerland)*, *12*(4), p. 1183. http://doi.org/10.3390/W12041183.

Grey, D., & Sadoff, C. W. (2007). Sink or Swim? Water security for growth and development. *Water Policy*, *9*(6), pp. 545–571. http://doi.org/10.2166/wp.2007.021.

Grigg, N. S. (2014). The 2011–2012 drought in the United States: New lessons from a record event. *International Journal of Water Resources Development*, *30*(2), pp. 183–199. http://doi.org/10.1080/07900627.2013.847710.

Grigg, N. S. (2021). Fifty years of water research: Has it made a difference? *Water International*, *46*(7–8), pp. 1087–1098. http://doi.org/10.1080/02508060.2021.1996968.

Heisler, J., Glibert, P. M., Burkholder, J. M., et al. (2008). Eutrophication and harmful algal blooms: A scientific consensus. *Harmful Algae*, *8*(1), pp. 3–13. http://doi.org/10.1016/j.hal.2008.08.006.

Hering, D., Borja, A., Carstensen, J., et al. (2010). The European Water Framework Directive at the age of 10: A critical review of the achievements with recommendations for the future. *Science of the Total Environment, 408* (19), pp. 4007–4019. http://doi.org/10.1016/j.scitotenv.2010.05.031.

Herrfahrdt-Pähle, E. (2014). Applying the concept of fit to water governance reforms in South Africa. *Ecology and Society, 19*(1), p. 25. http://doi.org/10.5751/ES-05964-190125.

Heyd, H., & Neef, A. (2006). Public participation in water management in northern Thai highlands. *Water Policy, 8*(5), pp. 395–413. http://doi.org/10.2166/wp.2006.048.

Hoekstra, A. Y., & Chapagain, A. K. (2011). *Globalization of Water: Sharing the Planet's Freshwater Resources*. New York: John Wiley & Sons.

Holley, C., & Sincalir, D. (2013). Deliberative participation, environmental law and collaborative governance: Insights from surface and groundwater studies. *Environmental and Planning Law Journal, 30*(32), pp. 32–55. www.researchgate.net/publication/287575180.

Hove, J., D'Ambruoso, L., Mabetha, D., et al. (2019). 'Water is life': Developing community participation for clean water in rural South Africa. *BMJ Global Health, 4*(3), e001377. http://doi.org/10.1136/bmjgh-2018-001377.

Imperial, M. T. (2005). Using collaboration as a governance strategy: Lessons from six watershed management programs. *Administration and Society, 37* (3), pp. 281–320. http://doi.org/10.1177/0095399705276111.

IPCC (2023). *Climate Change 2023: Synthesis Report.* Contribution of Working Groups I, II and III to the Sixth Assessment Report of the Intergovernmental Panel on Climate Change. Core Writing Team: H. Lee & J. Romero (eds.). Geneva: IPCC, pp. 35–115. http://doi.prg/10.59327/IPCC/AR6-9789291691647.

Ireland, J. D. (2007). *Udana and the Itivuttaka: Two Classics from the Pali Canon*. Kandy: Buddhist Publication Society. ISBN 978-955-24-0164-0.

Islam, M. S., Ahmed, M. K., Raknuzzaman, M., Habibullah-Al-Mamun, M., & Islam, M. K. (2015). Heavy metal pollution in surface water and sediment: a preliminary assessment of an urban river in a developing country. *Ecological indicators, 48*, pp. 282–291. http://doi.org/10.1016/j.ecolind.2014.08.016.

Jackson, S., & Barber, M. (2013). Recognition of indigenous water values in Australia's Northern Territory: Current progress and ongoing challenges for social justice in water planning. *Planning Theory and Practice, 14*(4), pp. 435–454. http://doi.org/10.1080/14649357.2013.845684.

Jetoo, S. (2018). Multi-level governance innovations of the Baltic Sea and the North American Great Lakes: New actors and their roles in building adaptive capacity for eutrophication governance. *Marine Policy*, *98*, pp. 237–245. http://doi.org/10.1016/j.marpol.2018.09.020.

Jetoo, S., & Krantzberg, G. (2016). Adaptive capacity for eutrophication governance of the laurentian great lakes. *Electronic Green Journal*, *1*(39). http://doi.org/10.5070/g313927488.

Jiang, Y., Zevenbergen, C., & Fu, D. (2017). Understanding the challenges for the governance of China's 'sponge cities' initiative to sustainably manage urban stormwater and flooding. *Natural Hazards*, *89*(1), pp. 521–529. http://doi.org/10.1007/s11069-017-2977-1.

Jury, W. A., & Vaux, H. (2005). The role of science in solving the world's emerging water problems. *The Proceedings of the National Academy of Sciences*, *102*(44), pp. 15715–15720. www.pnas.org/doi/pdf/10.1073/pnas.0506467102.

Jury, W. A., & Vaux, H. J. (2007). The emerging global water crisis: Managing scarcity and conflict between water users. *Advances in Agronomy*, *95*, pp. 1–76. http://doi.org/10.1016/50065-2113(07)95001-4.

Kastens, B., & Newig, J. (2008). Will participation foster the successful implementation of the water framework directive? The case of agricultural groundwater protection in northwest Germany. *Local Environment*, *13*(1), pp. 27–41. http://doi.org/10.1080/13549830701581713.

Khan, S., Hanjra, M. A., & Mu, J. (2009). Water management and crop production for food security in China: A review. *Agricultural Water Management*, *96*(3), pp. 349–360. http://doi.org/10.1016/j.agwat.2008.09.022.

Kirschke, S., Borchardt, D., & Newig, J. (2017). Mapping complexity in environmental governance: A comparative analysis of 37 priority issues in German water management. *Environmental Policy and Governance*, *27*(6), pp. 534–559. http://doi.org/10.1002/eet.1778.

Kirschke, S., Häger, A., Kirschke, D., & Völker, J. (2019). Agricultural nitrogen pollution of freshwater in Germany: The governance of sustaining a complex problem. *Water*, *11*(12), 2450. http://doi.org/10.3390/w11122450.

Kirschke, S., Newig, J., Völker, J., & Borchardt, D. (2017). Does problem complexity matter for environmental policy delivery? How public authorities address problems of water governance. *Journal of Environmental Management*, *196*, pp. 1–7. https://doi.org/10.1016/j.jenvman.2017.02.068.

Koehler, J. K. L. (2023). Not all risks are equal: A risk governance framework for assessing the water SDG. *International Environmental Agreements: Politics, Law, and Economics*, *23*(2), pp. 179–189. http://doi.org/10.1007/s10784-023-09617-7.

Kummu, M., Ward, P. J., de Moel, H., & Varis, O. (2010). Is physical water scarcity a new phenomenon? Global assessment of water shortage over the last two millennia. *Environmental Research Letters*, *5*(3). http://doi.org/10.1088/1748-9326/5/3/034006.

Lach, D., Rayner, S., & Ingram, H. (2005). Taming the waters: Strategies to domesticate the wicked problems of water resource management. *International Journal of Water*, *3*(1), pp. 1–17. http://doi.org/10.1504/IJW.2005.007156.

Lautze, J., de Silva, S., Giordano, M., & Sanford, L. (2011). Putting the cart before the horse: Water governance and IWRM. *Natural Resources Forum*, *35*(1), pp. 1–8. http://doi.org/10.1111/j.1477-8947.2010.01339.x.

Leal, P. A. (2007). Participation: The ascendancy of a buzzword in the neo-liberal era. *Development in Practice*, *17*(4–5), pp. 539–548. http://doi.org/10.1080/09614520701469518.

Leduc, C., Pulido-Bosch, A., & Remini, B. (2017). Anthropization of groundwater resources in the Mediterranean region: Processes and challenges. *Hydrogeology Journal*, *25*(6), pp. 1529–1547. http://doi.org/10.1007/s10040-017-1572-6.

Lee, F., & Moss, T. (2014). Spatial fit and water politics: managing asymmetries in the Dongjiang River basin. *International Journal of River Basin Management*, *12*(4), pp. 329–339. http://doi.org/10.1080/15715124.2014.917420.

Li, E., Endter-Wada, J., & Li, S. (2015). Characterizing and contextualizing the water challenges of megacities. *Journal of the American Water Resources Association*, *51*(3), pp. 589–613. http://doi.org/10.1111/1752-1688.12310.

Li, T. H. Y., Ng, S. T., & Skitmore, M. (2013). Evaluating stakeholder satisfaction during public participation in major infrastructure and construction projects: A fuzzy approach. *Automation in Construction*, *29*, pp. 123–135. http://doi.org/10.1016/j.autcon.2012.09.007.

Liebenguth, J. (2020). Conceptions of security in global environmental discourses: Exploring the water–energy–food security nexus. *Critical Studies on Security*, *8*(3), pp. 189–202. http://doi.org/10.1080/21624887.2020.1754713.

Lienert, J., Schnetzer, F., & Ingold, K. (2013). Stakeholder analysis combined with social network analysis provides fine-grained insights into water infrastructure planning processes. *Journal of Environmental Management*, *125*, pp. 134–148. http://doi.org/10.1016/j.jenvman.2013.03.052.

Linton, J. (2010). *What Is Water?: The History of a Modern Abstraction*. Vancouver: University of British Columbia Press.

Lopus, S., McCord, P., Gower, D., & Evans, T. (2017). Drivers of farmer satisfaction with small-scale irrigation systems. *Applied Geography*, *89*, pp. 77–86. http://doi.org/10.1016/j.apgeog.2017.10.004.

Lynch, A. H., Griggs, D., Joachim, L., & Walker, J. (2013). The role of the Yorta Yorta people in clarifying the common interest in sustainable management of the Murray–Darling Basin, Australia. *Policy Sciences, 46*(2), pp. 109–123. http://doi.org/10.1007/s11077-012-9164-8.

Maas, B., Pakeman, R. J., Godet, L., et al. (2021). Women and Global South strikingly underrepresented among top-publishing ecologists. *Conservation Letters, 14*(4), e12797. https://doi.org/10.1111/conl.12797.

Macura-Nnamdi, E., & Sikora, T. (2023). WATER. *Angelaki, 28*(1), pp. 3–8. https://doi.org/10.1080/0969725X.2023.2167778.

Mancosu, N., Snyder, R. L., Kyriakakis, G., & Spano, D. (2015). Water scarcity and future challenges for food production. *Water (Switzerland), 7*(3), pp. 975–992. http://doi.org/10.3390/w7030975.

Markowska, J., Szalińska, W., Dąbrowska, J., & Brząkała, M. (2020). The concept of a participatory approach to water management on a reservoir in response to wicked problems. *Journal of Environmental Management, 259*, 109626. http://doi.org/10.1016/j.jenvman.2019.109626.

McCormick, A., Hoellein, T. J., Mason, S. A., Schluep, J., & Kelly, J. J. (2014). Microplastic is an abundant and distinct microbial habitat in an urban river. *Environmental Science & Technology, 48*(20), pp. 11863–11871. https://doi.org/10.1021/es503610r.

McDonald, R. I., Weber, K., Padowski, J., et al. (2014). Water on an urban planet: Urbanization and the reach of urban water infrastructure. *Global Environmental Change, 27*(1), pp. 96–105. http://doi.org/10.1016/j.gloenvcha.2014.04.022.

McGhee, G., Marland, G. R., & Atkinson, J. (2007). Grounded theory research: Literature reviewing and reflexivity. *Journal of Advanced Nursing, 60*(3), pp. 334–342. http://doi.org/10.1111/j.1365-2648.2007.04436.x.

Medema, W., McIntosh, B. S., & Jeffrey, P. J. (2008). From premise to practice: A critical assessment of integrated water resources management and adaptive management approaches in the water sector. *Ecology and Society, 13*(2), p. 29. http://doi.org/10.5751/ES-02611-130229.

Mehta, L. & Nicol, A. (May 11, 2023). *How the UN Got Thirsty Again after 46 years*. Institute of Development Studies. www.ids.ac.uk/opinions/how-the-un-got-thirsty-again-after-46-years/.

Mekonnen, M. M., & Hoekstra, A. Y. (2016). Sustainability: Four billion people facing severe water scarcity. *Science Advances, 2*(2). http://doi.org/10.1126/sciadv.1500323.

Memon, S., Umrani, S., & Pathan, H. (2017). Application of constant comparison method in social sciences: A useful technique to analyze interviews.

Grassroots, *51*(1), pp. 152–165. www.researchgate.net/publication/355734488.

Miranda, J. J., & Zaman, M. J. (2010). Exporting 'failure': Why research from rich countries may not benefit the developing world. *Revista de saúde pública*, *44*, pp. 185–189. http://doi.org/10.1590/s0034-89102010000100020.

Mishra, A. K., & Singh, V. P. (2010). A review of drought concepts. *Journal of Hydrology*, *391*(1–2), pp. 202–216. http://doi.org/10.1016/j.jhydrol.2010.07.012.

Moe, C. L., & Rheingans, R. D. (2006). Global challenges in water, sanitation and health. *Journal of Water and Health*, *4*, pp. 41–57. http://doi.org/10.2166/wh.2005.039.

Moher, D., Shamseer, L., Clarke, M., et al. (2015). Preferred reporting items for systematic review and meta-analysis protocols (PRISMA-P) 2015 statement. *Revista Espanola de Nutricion Humana y Dietetica*, *20*(2), pp. 148–160. http://doi.org/10.1186/2046-4053-4-1.

Molenveld, A., & van Buuren, A. (2019). Flood risk and resilience in the Netherlands: In search of an adaptive governance approach. *Water (Switzerland)*, *11*(12), 2563. http://doi.org/10.3390/w11122563.

Molle, F., & Berkoff, J. (2009). Cities vs. agriculture: A review of intersectoral water re-allocation. *Natural Resources Forum*, *33*(1), pp. 6–18. http://doi.org/10.1111/j.1477-8947.2009.01204.x.

Molle, F., Lankford, B., & Lave, R. (2024). Water and the politics of quantification: A programmatic review. *Water Alternatives*, *17*(2), pp. 325–347.

Montgomery, M. A., & Elimelech, M. (2007). Water and sanitation in developing countries: Including health in the equation. *Environmental Science & Technology*, *41*, pp. 17–24.

Moss, T. (2012). Spatial fit, from panacea to practice: Implementing the EU water framework directive. *Ecology and Society*, *17*(3), p. 2. http://doi.org/10.5751/ES-04821-170302.

Motta-Veiga, M. (2021). Tariff structuring in water and sanitation: Public profiting arrangements on universalization initiatives. *Water Policy*, *23*(3), pp. 599–616. http://doi.org/10.2166/wp.2021.082.

Mvungi, A., Mashauri, D., & Madulu, N. F. (2005). Management of water for irrigation agriculture in semi-arid areas: Problems and prospects. *Physics and Chemistry of the Earth*, *30*(11–16), pp. 809–817. http://doi.org/10.1016/j.pce.2005.08.024.

Nature Index (2024). 2024 research leaders: Leading countries/territories in natural sciences. www.nature.com/nature-index/research-leaders/2024/country/all/global.

Nature Sustainability Editorial Board (2021). Too much and not enough. *Nature Sustainability*, *4*(8), p. 659. https://doi.org/10.1038/s41893-021-00766-8.

Neto, S. (2016). Water governance in an urban age. *Utilities Policy*, *43*, pp. 32–41. http://doi.org/10.1016/j.jup.2016.05.004.

Ngure, F. M., Reid, B. M., Humphrey, J. H., Mbuya, M. N., Pelto, G., & Stoltzfus, R. J. (2014). Water, sanitation, and hygiene (WASH), environmental enteropathy, nutrition, and early child development: Making the links. *Annals of the New York Academy of Sciences*, *1308*(1), pp. 118–128. http://doi.org/10.1111/nyas.12330.

Nielsen, M. W., & Andersen, J. P. (2021). Global citation inequality is on the rise. *Proceedings of the National Academy of Sciences*, 118(7), e2012208118.

North, M. A., Hastie, W. W., & Hoyer, L. (2020). Out of Africa: The underrepresentation of African authors in high-impact geoscience literature. *Earth-Science Reviews*, *208*, 103262. http://doi.org/10.1590/s0034-89102010000100020.

Obeng-Odoom, F. (2012). Beyond access to water. *Development in Practice*, *22*(8), pp. 1135–1146. http://doi.org/10.1080/09614524.2012.714744.

Oki, T., & Kanae, S. (2006). Global hydrological cycles and world water resources. *New Series*, *313*(5790). http://doi.org/10.1126/science.1128845.

Onwuegbuzie, A. J., Leech, N. L., & Collins, K. M. T. (2012). Qualitative analysis techniques for the review of the literature. *Qualitative Report*, *17*(28). http://doi.org/10.46743/2160-3715/2012.1754.

Ostrom, E. (2008). The challenge of common-pool resources. *Environment: Science and Policy for Sustainable Development*, *50*(4), pp. 8–21. https://doi.org/10.3200/ENVT.50.4.8-21.

Ouyang, Z., Zheng, H., Xiao, Y., et al. (2016). Improvements in ecosystem services from investments in natural capital. *Science*, *352*(6292), pp. 1455–1459. http://doi.org/10.1126/science.aaf2295.

Ozbekhan, H. (1970). *The Predicament of Mankind: A Quest for Structured Responses to Growing World-Wide Complexities and Uncertainties. Proposal to the Club of Rome*. New York: The Club of Rome.

Özerol, G., Bressers, H., & Coenen, F. (2012). Irrigated agriculture and environmental sustainability: An alignment perspective. *Environmental Science and Policy*, *23*, pp. 57–67. http://doi.org/10.1016/j.envsci.2012.07.015.

Pahl-Wostl, C. (2017). An evolutionary perspective on water governance: From understanding to transformation. *Water Resources Management*, *31*(10), pp. 2917–2932. http://doi.org/10.1007/s11269-017-1727-1.

Pahl-Wostl, C. (2019). Governance of the water-energy-food security nexus: A multi-level coordination challenge. *Environmental Science and Policy*, *92*, pp. 356–367. http://doi.org/10.1016/j.envsci.2017.07.017.

Pahl-Wostl, C., Craps, M., Dewulf, A., Mostert, E., Tabara, D., & Taillieu, T. (2007). Social learning and water resources management. *Ecology and Society*, *12*(2), p. 5. www.ecologyandsociety.org/vol12/iss2/art5/.

Pahl-Wostl, C., Gupta, J., & Petry, D. (2008). Governance and the global water system: A theoretical exploration. *Global Governance*, *14*(4), pp. 419–435. www.jstor.org/stable/27800722.

Pahl-Wostl, C., & Knieper, C. (2014). The capacity of water governance to deal with the climate change adaptation challenge: Using fuzzy set qualitative comparative analysis to distinguish between polycentric, fragmented, and centralized regimes. *Global Environmental Change*, *29*, pp. 139–154. http://doi.org/10.1016/j.gloenvcha.2014.09.003.

Patterson, J. J. (2016). Exploring local responses to a wicked problem: Context, collective action, and outcomes in catchments in subtropical Australia. *Society and Natural Resources*, *29*(10), pp. 1198–1213. http://doi.org/10.1080/08941920.2015.1132353.

Patterson, J. J., Smith, C., & Bellamy, J. (2015). Enabling and enacting 'practical action' in catchments: Responding to the 'wicked problem' of nonpoint source pollution in coastal subtropical Australia. *Environmental Management*, *55*(2), pp. 479–495. http://doi.org/10.1007/s00267-014-0409-5.

Pimentel, D., Berger, B., Filiberto, D., et al. (2004). Water resources – agricultural and environmental issues. *BioScience*, *54*(10), pp. 909–918. http://doi.org/10.1641/0006-3568(2004)054[0909:WRAAEI]2.0.CO;2.

Prüss-Ustün, A., Wolf, J., Bartram, J., et al. (2019). Burden of disease from inadequate water, sanitation and hygiene for selected adverse health outcomes: An updated analysis with a focus on low- and middle-income countries. *International Journal of Hygiene and Environmental Health*, *222*(5), pp. 765–777. http://doi.org/10.1016/j.ijheh.2019.05.004.

Puy, A., & Lankford, B. A. (2024). The water crisis by the Global Commission on the Economics of Water: A totalising narrative built on shaky numbers. *Water Alternatives*, *17*(2): pp. 369–390.

Qiu, J., Wardropper, C. B., Rissman, A. R., & Turner, M. G. (2017). Spatial fit between water quality policies and hydrologic ecosystem services in an urbanizing agricultural landscape. *Landscape Ecology*, *32*(1), pp. 59–75. http://doi.org/10.1007/s10980-016-0428-0.

Quentin Grafton, R., Biswas, A. K., Bosch, H., et al. (2023). Goals, progress and priorities from Mar del Plata in 1977 to New York in 2023. *Nature Water*, *1*(3), 230–240. https://doi.org/10.1038/s44221-023-00041-4.

Querejazu, A. (2022). Water governance. *New Perspectives*, *30*(2), pp. 180–188. http://doi.org/10.1177/2336825X221089189.

Rana, M. M. P., & Piracha, A. (2018). Supplying water to the urban poor: Processes and challenges of community-based water governance in Dhaka city. *Management of Environmental Quality: An International Journal, 29* (4), pp. 608–622. http://doi.org/10.1108/MEQ-11-2017-0127.

Rangecroft, S., Rohse, M., Banks, E. W., et al. (2021). Guiding principles for hydrologists conducting interdisciplinary research and fieldwork with participants. *Hydrological Sciences Journal, 66*(2), pp. 214–225. http://doi.org/10.1080/02626667.2020.1852241.

Reichenberger, S., Bach, M., Skitschak, A., & Frede, H. G. (2007). Mitigation strategies to reduce pesticide inputs into ground-and surface water and their effectiveness; a review. *Science of the Total Environment, 384*(1–3), pp. 1–35. https://doi.org/10.1016/j.scitotenv.2007.04.046.

Richey, A. S., Thomas, B. F., Lo, M. H., et al. (2015). Quantifying renewable groundwater stress with GRACE. *Water Resources Research, 51*(7), pp. 5217–5237. http://doi.org/10.1002/2015WR017349.

Rijke, J., Farrelly, M., Brown, R., & Zevenbergen, C. (2013). Configuring transformative governance to enhance resilient urban water systems. *Environmental Science and Policy, 25*, pp. 62–72. http://doi.org/10.1016/j.envsci.2012.09.012.

Rijsberman, F. R. (2006). Water scarcity: Fact or fiction? *Agricultural Water Management, 80*(1–3), pp. 5–22. http://doi.org/10.1016/j.agwat.2005.07.001.

Rittel, H. W. J., & Webber, M. M. (1973). Dilemmas in a general theory of planning. *Policy Sciences, 4*, pp. 155–169. https://doi.org/10.1007/BF01405730.

Roca, E. & Anand Tularam, G. (2012). Which way does water flow? An econometric analysis of the global price integration of water stocks. *Applied Economics, 44*(23), pp. 2935–2944. http://doi.org/10.1080/00036846.2011.568403.

Rodriguez, D. J., van den Berg, C. & McMahon, A. (2012). *Investing in Water Infrastructure: Capital, Operations and Maintenance.* Washington, DC: The World Bank.

Rogers, P., & Hall, A. W. (2003). *Effective Water Governance.* Stockholm: Global Water Partnership TEC Background Papers No. 7.

Rojas, D. R., & Postigo, J. C. (2025). The cycle of underrepresentation: structural and institutional factors limiting the representation of Global South authors and knowledge in the IPCC. *Climatic Change, 178*(2), 19. https://doi.org/10.1007/s10584-025-03857-z.

Romm, J., Conrad, E., & Måren, I. E. (2018). Resilient governance of water regimes in variable climates: Lessons from California's hydro-ecological zones. *Water (Switzerland), 10*(2), 196. http://doi.org/10.3390/w10020196.

Roque, A., Wutich, A., Quimby, B., et al. (2022). Participatory approaches in water research: A review. *Wiley Interdisciplinary Reviews: Water*, *9*((2), e1577. http://doi.org/10.1002/wat2.1577.

Roth, D., Vink, M., Warner, J., & Winnubst, M. (2017). Watered-down politics? Inclusive water governance in the Netherlands. *Ocean and Coastal Management*, *150*, pp. 51–61. http://doi.org/10.1016/j.ocecoaman.2017.02.020.

Rulli, M. C., Saviori, A., & D'Odorico, P. (2013). Global land and water grabbing. *Proceedings of the National Academy of Sciences*, *110*(3), pp. 892–897. https://doi.org/10.1073/pnas.1213163110.

Sanya, T. (2020). Freshwater: Towards a better understanding of a wicked problem. *International Journal of Environmental Science & Sustainable Development*, *5*(2), pp. 48–59. http://doi.org/10.21625/essd.v5i2.759.

Schindler, D. W. (2006). Recent advances in the understanding and management of eutrophication. *Limnology and Oceanography*, *51*(1 II), pp. 356–363. http://doi.org/10.4319/lo.2006.51.1_part_2.0356.

Shankar, P. S. V., Kulkarni, H., & Krishnan, S. (2011). India's groundwater challenge. *Economic & Political Weekly*, *46*(2), pp. 37–45. www.jstor.org/stable/27918012.

Sheffield, J., Wood, E. F., & Roderick, M. L. (2012). Little change in global drought over the past 60 years. *Nature*, *491*(7424), pp. 435–438. http://doi.org/10.1038/nature11575.

Silveti, D., & Andersson, K. (2019). Challenges of governing off-grid 'productive' sanitation in peri-urban areas: Comparison of case studies in Bolivia and South Africa. *Sustainability (Switzerland)*, *11*(12), 3468. http://doi.org/10.3390/SU11123468.

Sivapalan, M., Savenije, H. H., & Bloschl, G. (2012). Socio-hydrology: A new science of people and water. *Hydrological Processes*, *26*, pp. 1270–1276. http://doi.org/10.1002/hyp.8426.

Sixt, G. N., Klerkx, L., Aiken, J. D., & Griffin, T. S. (2019). Nebraska's Natural Resource District system: Collaborative approaches to adaptive groundwater quality governance. *Water Alternatives*, *12*(2), pp. 676–698. www.water-alternatives.org/index.php/alldoc/articles/vol12/v12issue2/498-a12-2-5/file.

Short, A. G. (2013). Governing change: Land-use change and the prevention of nonpoint source pollution in the north coastal basin of California. *Environmental Management*, *51*(1), pp. 108–125. http://doi.org/10.1007/s00267-011-9729-x.

Sojamo, S. & Rudebeck, T. (2024). Corporate engagement in water policy and governance: A literature review on water stewardship and water security. *Water Alternatives*, *17*(2), pp. 292–324.

References

Solanes, M., & Gonzalez-Villarreal, F. (1999). *The Dublin Principles for Water as Reflected in a Comparative Assessment of Institutional and Legal Arrangements for Integrated Water Resources Management.* Global Water Partnership Technical Advisory Committee, Santiago, Chile GOZ (1998) Water Bill, draft, Ministry of Rural Resource and Water Development. Rural Water Supply and Sanitation–Review of the IRWSSP, 2.

Souvik Ghosh, S., Singh, R., Kundu, D. K., & Kumar, A. (2008). Farmers' participation in irrigation management. *Journal of Rural Development, 27* (2), pp. 231–244. www.researchgate.net/publication/288224524.

Srinivasan, V., Lambin, E.F., Gorelick, S.M., Thompson, B.H., & Rozelle, S. (2012). The nature and causes of the global water crisis: Syndromes from a meta-analysis of coupled human–water studies. *Water Resources Research, 48*(10). http://doi.org/10.1029/2011WR011087.

Srinivasan, V., Seto, K. C., Emerson, R., & Gorelick, S. M. (2013). The impact of urbanization on water vulnerability: A coupled human-environment system approach for Chennai, India. *Global Environmental Change, 23*(1), pp. 229–239. http://doi.org/10.1016/j.gloenvcha.2012.10.002.

Su, L., Xue, Y., Li, L., et al. (2016). Microplastics in taihu lake, China. *Environmental Pollution, 216,* pp. 711–719. http://doi.org/10.1016/j.envpol.2016.06.036.

Sun, B., Zhang, L., Yang, L., et al. (2012). Agricultural non-point source pollution in China: Causes and mitigation measures. *Ambio, 41*(4), pp. 370–379. http://doi.org/10.1007/s13280-012-0249-6.

te Wierik, S. A., Gupta, J., Cammeraat, E. L. H., & Artzy-Randrup, Y. A. (2020). The need for green and atmospheric water governance. *Wiley Interdisciplinary Reviews: Water, 7*(2), e1406. http://doi.org/10.1002/wat2.1406.

Toure, N. M., Kane, A., Noel, J. F., et al. (2012). Water-poverty relationships in the coastal town of Mbour (Senegal): Relevance of GIS for decision support. *International Journal of Applied Earth Observation and Geoinformation, 14* (1), pp. 33–39. http://doi.org/10.1016/j.jag.2011.08.001.

van der Zaag, P., Gupta, J., & Darvis, L. P. (2009). HESS Opinions 'Urgent water challenges are not sufficiently researched.' *Hydrology and Earth System Sciences, 13,* pp. 905–912. www.hydrol-earth-syst-sci.net/13/905/2009/.

Vásquez, W. F., & Franceschi, D. (2013). System reliability and water service decentralization: Investigating household preferences in Nicaragua. *Water Resources Management, 27*(14), pp. 4913–4926. http://doi.org/10.1007/s11269-013-0447-4.

Venot, J. P., Vos, J., Molle, F., et al. (2022). A bridge over troubled waters. *Nature Sustainability, 5*(2), p. 92. http://doi.org/10.1038/s41893-021-00835-y.

Vinciguerra, T. (2024). Water as a common good? Academic differences and their impact on the 2023 United Nations Water Conference. *Water Policy*, wp2024131. https://doi.org/10.2166/wp.2024.131.

Vörösmarty, C. J., McIntyre, P. B., Gessner, M. O., et al. (2010). Global threats to human water security and river biodiversity. *Nature*, *467*(7315), pp. 555–561. http://doi.org/10.1038/nature09440.

Voulvoulis, N., Arpon, K. D., & Giakoumis, T. (2017). The EU Water Framework Directive: From great expectations to problems with implementation. *Science of The Total Environment*, *575*, pp. 358–366. http://doi.org/10.1016/j.scitotenv.2016.09.228.

Wada, Y., & Bierkens, M. F. P. (2014). Sustainability of global water use: Past reconstruction and future projections. *Environmental Research Letters*, *9*(10). http://doi.org/10.1088/1748-9326/9/10/104003.

Wada, Y., van Beek, L. P. H., van Kempen, C. M., et al. (2010). Global depletion of groundwater resources. *Geophysical Research Letters*, *37*(20). http://doi.org/10.1029/2010GL044571.

Webber, M., Barnet, J., Chen, Z., et al. (2015). Constructing water shortages on a huge river: The case of Shanghai. *Geographical Research*, *53*(4), pp. 406–418. http://doi.org/10.1111/1745-5871.12132.

Wehn, U., Rusca, M., Evers, J., & Lanfranchi, V. (2015). Participation in flood risk management and the potential of citizen observatories: A governance analysis. *Environmental Science and Policy*, *48*, pp. 225–236. http://doi.org/10.1016/j.envsci.2014.12.017.

Wheater, H. S., & Gober, P. (2015). Water security and the science agenda. *Water Resources Research*, *51*(7), pp. 5406–5424. http://doi.org/10.1002/2015WR016892.

Wiering, M., Liefferink, D., Boezeman, D., et al. (2020). The wicked problem the water framework directive cannot solve: The governance approach in dealing with pollution of nutrients in surface water in the Netherlands, Flanders, Lower Saxony, Denmark and Ireland. *Water*, *12*(5), 1240. http://doi.org/10.3390/w12041240.

Wilk, J., Rydhagen, B., Jonsson, A. C., et al. (2017). Framing and blaming in the Cochabamba water agenda: Local, municipal, and regional perspectives. *Water Policy*, *19*(4), pp. 620–636. http://doi.org/10.2166/wp.2017.050.

Wolf, A. T. (2007). Shared waters: Conflict and cooperation. *Annual Review of Environment and Resources*, *32*, pp. 241–269. http://doi.org/10.1146/annurev.energy.32.041006.101434.

Woodhouse, P., & Muller, M. (2017). Water governance: An historical perspective on current debates. *World Development*, *92*, pp. 225–241. http://doi.org/10.1016/j.worlddev.2016.11.014.

Wu, Y., & Chen, J. (2013). Investigating the effects of point source and nonpoint source pollution on the water quality of the East River (Dongjiang) in South China. *Ecological Indicators*, *32*, pp. 294–304. https://doi.org/10.1016/j.ecolind.2013.04.002.

Yates, D., Sieber, J., Purkey, D., & Huber-Lee, A. (2005). WEAP21 – A demand-, priority-, and preference-driven water planning model. Part 1: Model characteristics. *Water International*, *30*(4), pp. 487–500. http://doi.org/10.1080/02508060508691893.

Zegwaard, A., & Wester, P. (2014). Inside matters of facts: Reopening dams and debates in the Netherlands. *Water Alternatives*, *7*(3), pp. 464–479.

Zhang, H. (2016). Sino-Indian water disputes: The coming water wars? *Wiley Interdisciplinary Reviews: Water*, *3*(2), pp. 155–166. https://doi.org/10.1002/wat2.1123.

Zhao, J. Z., Fonseca, C., & Zeerak, R. (2019). Stormwater utility fees and credits: A funding strategy for Sustainability. *Sustainability (Switzerland)*, *11*(7), 1913. http://doi.org/10.3390/su11071913.

Zingraff-Hamed, A., Schröter, B., Schaub, S., et al. (2020). Perception of bottlenecks in the implementation of the European Water Framework Directive. *Water Alternatives* *13*(3), pp. 458–483.

Zwarteveen, M., Kemerink-Seyoum, J. S., Kooy, M., et al. (2017). Engaging with the politics of water governance. *Wiley Interdisciplinary Reviews: Water*, *4*(6), pp. 1–9. http://doi.org/10.1002/wat2.1245.

Acknowledgments

The authors would like to thank the Editor-in-Chief and the anonymous reviewers for their valuable comments. This publication acknowledges funding from the European Union's Horizon 2020 research and innovation programme under the Marie Skłodowska-Curie Innovative Training Network NEWAVE – grant agreement No. 861509.

Cambridge Elements

Sustainability: Science, Policy, Practice

Editor-in-Chief

Arun Agrawal
University of Notre Dame

Arun Agrawal is the Pulte Family Professor of Development Policy at the Keough School of Global Affairs and the inaugural director of the Just Transformations to Sustainability Initiative at the University of Notre Dame. His research focuses on the political economy of human-environment interactions and systems, sustainability of social-ecological systems, governance of natural resources, inter-temporal and cross-scale dynamics of socio-environmental changes, and the relationship of climate and environmental stressors with conflict, inequality, and health.

Advisory Editorial Board

Neil Adger, *University of Exeter*
Anthony Bebbington, *The Ford Foundation*
Christoph Bene, *Alliance Bioversity International*
William Clark, *Harvard University*
Ruth S. DeFries, *Columbia University*
Melissa Leach, *University of Sussex*
Diana Liverman, *University of Arizona*
Yadvinder Malhi, *University of Oxford*
Debra Rowe, *Oakland Community College*
B. L. Turner II, *Arizona State University*
Esther Turnhout, *University of Twente*

Editorial Board

Vanesa Castan Broto, *The University of Sheffield*
Paul J. Ferraro, *Johns Hopkins University*
Reetika Khera, *Indian Institute of Technology Delhi*
Myanna Lahsen, *Linkoping University*
Christian Lund, *University of Copenhagen*
Johan Oldekop, *University of Manchester*
Laura Vang Rasmussen, *University of Copenhagen*
Diana Ürge-Vorsatz, *Central European University*

About the Series

This series showcases scholarship that investigates persistent, multi-scale challenges to global sustainability. It facilitates the consolidation of the science and social science of sustainability, bridging the gap between knowledge, policy, and practice. It aims to include the best reviews of relevant themes related to environment, development, and sustainability.

Cambridge Elements

Sustainability: Science, Policy, Practice

Elements in the Series

Girl Power: Sustainability, Empowerment, and Justice
Jin In

Climate Change on Trial
César Rodríguez-Garavito

How To Normatively Transform Food Systems
Abdul-Rahim Abdulai and Christophe Béné

*A Bit Too Simple: Narratives of Development,
Sustainability and Climate Change*
Mette Fog Olwig

On the Global Water Crisis: A Taxonomy of Human–Water Challenges
Paulina Raniecka, Nikolas Galli, Camilla Govoni, Maria Cristina Rulli,
Sergio Villamayor-Tomas, and Jampel Dell'Angelo

A full series listing is available at: www.cambridge.org/ESBL

For EU product safety concerns, contact us at Calle de José Abascal, 56–1°,
28003 Madrid, Spain or eugpsr@cambridge.org.

www.ingramcontent.com/pod-product-compliance
Ingram Content Group UK Ltd.
Pitfield, Milton Keynes, MK11 3LW, UK
UKHW020954250326
469333UK00018B/646